GEORG BÜCHNER

Georg Büchner was born in 1813 in Goddelau, Germany, into
a family of doctors. He studied Zoology and Anatomy at the
University of Strasbourg, and was appointed lecturer at the
University of Zürich in 1836. However, his main passion was for
politics. During a year 'out' at Giessen University, he joined the
radical movement known as 'Young Germany', co-founded the
grandly-named Secret Society for the Rights of Man, and was
one of the authors of a pamphlet (*The Hessian Courier*) which
urged working people of Hesse, his native part of Germany, to
win social rights by force. His co-authors of this document were
arrested and imprisoned. Büchner escaped by denying any
involvement with the pamphlet, by accepting house-arrest at his
parents' home, and then by leaving Germany forever.

In 1835, penniless and on the run from the secret police,
Büchner wrote his first play, *Danton's Death*, about the despair
and disillusion felt by Danton, the French Revolutionary leader
whose colleagues turned on him, rejected his ideals and
condemned him to the guillotine. In 1836, when he was under
house-arrest, he wrote (for a prize competition) *Leonce and
Lena*, about a prince and princess who decide to rescue their
country from aristocratic corruption and make it an ideal state.

Büchner contracted typhus and died at the age of twenty-four in
February 1837, leaving his third and most famous play, *Woyzeck*,
unfinished. Based on the real-life case history of Johann Christian
Woyzeck, who was arrested for stabbing to death his lover, Frau
Woost, in 1821, *Woyzeck* has been 'completed' by many authors,
translators and editors, and has become one of the most
performed and influential plays in German theatre.

JACK THORNE

Jack Thorne's plays for the stage include *Junkyard* (Headlong/
Bristol Old Vic/Rose Theatre Kingston/Theatr Clwyd); *Harry
Potter and the Cursed Child* (Palace Theatre, London, 2016);
The Solid Life of Sugar Water (Graeae Theatre Company); *Hope*
(Royal Court Theatre, London, 2014); adaptations of *Let the
Right One In* (National Theatre of Scotland at Dundee Rep, the
Royal Court and the Apollo Theatre, London, 2013/14) and
Stuart: A Life Backwards (Underbelly, Edinburgh, and tour,
2013); *Mydidae* (Soho, 2012; Trafalgar Studios, 2013); an
adaptation of Friedrich Dürrenmatt's *The Physicists* (Donmar
Warehouse, 2012); *Bunny* (Underbelly, Edinburgh, 2010; Soho,
2011); *2nd May 1997* (Bush, 2009); *Burying Your Brother in the
Pavement* (National Theatre Connections, 2008); *When You
Cure Me* (Bush, 2005; Radio 3's Drama on Three, 2006); *Fanny
and Faggot* (Pleasance, Edinburgh, 2004 and 2007; Finborough,
2007; English Theatre of Bruges, 2007; Trafalgar Studios,
2007); and *Stacy* (Tron, 2006; Arcola, 2007; Trafalgar Studios,
2007). His radio plays include *Left at the Angel* (Radio 4, 2007),
an adaptation of *The Hunchback of Notre Dame* (2009) and an
original play *People Snogging in Public Places* (Radio 3's Wire
slot, 2009). He was a core writer in all three series of *Skins* (E4,
Channel 4, BBC America), writing five episodes. His other TV
writing includes *National Treasure*, *The Last Panthers*, *Glue*,
The Fades (2012 BAFTA for Best Drama Series), *Shameless*,
Cast-Offs, *This is England '86* (2011 Royal Television Society
Award for Best Writer – Drama), *This is England '88*, *This is
England '90* and the thirty-minute drama *The Spastic King*. His
work for film includes the features *War Book*, *A Long Way
Down*, adapted from Nick Hornby's novel, and *The Scouting
Book for Boys*, which won him the Star of London Best
Newcomer Award at the London Film Festival 2009.

Georg Büchner

WOYZECK

in a new version by

Jack Thorne

NICK HERN BOOKS

London

www.nickhernbooks.co.uk

A Nick Hern Book

This version of *Woyzeck* first published as a paperback original in Great Britain in 2017 by Nick Hern Books Limited, The Glasshouse, 49a Goldhawk Road, London W12 8QP

Extract by John Berger: 'Prophet of a Pitiless World' (*Guardian*, 2004). Also published in *Portraits* (Verso Books, 2015). Reprinted with kind permission of the John Berger Estate

Cover artwork: AKSE P19/PENTAGRAM

Designed and typeset by Nick Hern Books, London
Printed in Great Britain by CPI Books (UK) Ltd

A CIP catalogue record for this book is available from the British Library

ISBN   978 1 84842 636 8

This version of *Woyzeck* premiered at The Old Vic theatre, London, on 15 May 2017, with the following cast:

ANDREWS	Ben Batt
WOYZECK	John Boyega
YOUNG WOYZECK	Carlo Brathwaite
MAGGIE/MOTHER	Nancy Carroll
DOCTOR MARTENS	Darrell D'Silva
MARIE	Sarah Greene
YOUNG WOYZECK	Reuel Guzman
GDR CITIZEN/ENSEMBLE	Isabella Marshall
YOUNG WOYZECK	Cyrus Odukale
CAPTAIN THOMPSON	Steffan Rhodri
LANDLORD/ENSEMBLE	David Rubin
EAST GERMAN SOLDIER/ ENSEMBLE	Theo Solomon

Director	Joe Murphy
Designer	Tom Scutt
Lighting Designer	Neil Austin
Sound Designer	Gareth Fry
Composer	Isobel Waller-Bridge
Movement Director	Polly Bennett
Illusion	Ben Hart
Fight Directors	Rachel Bown-Williams
	Ruth Cooper Brown
Casting Director	Jessica Ronane CDG

The author's proceeds from sales of this book and amateur licensing of the play will be donated to Young Minds, the charity committed to improving the emotional wellbeing and mental health of children and young people in the UK. youngminds.org.uk

'The present period of history is one of the Wall. When the Berlin one fell, the prepared plans to build walls everywhere were unrolled. Concrete, bureaucratic, surveillance, security, racist, zone walls. Everywhere the walls separate the desperate poor from those who hope against hope to stay relatively rich. The walls cross every sphere from crop cultivation to health care. They exist, too, in the richest metropolises of the world. The Wall is the front line of what, long ago, was called the class war.

...The choice of meaning in the world today is here between the two sides of the wall. The wall is also inside each one of us. Whatever our circumstances, we can choose within ourselves which side of the wall we are attuned to. It is not a wall between good and evil. Both exist on both sides. The choice is between self-respect and self-chaos.'

John Berger, 2004

For Cathy Mason

Characters

WOYZECK [Voy-tzeck], *British, early twenties*
MARIE, *Irish Catholic, early twenties*
ANDREWS, *British, late twenties/early thirties*
MAGGIE, *British, early forties*
MOTHER, *British, early forties*
CAPTAIN THOMPSON, *British, forties*
DOCTOR MARTENS, *German, forties*
YOUNG WOYZECK, *British, ten*

Also SINGER, GDR CITIZEN, EAST GERMAN SOLDIER,
  LANDLORD

MAGGIE *and* MOTHER *need to be played by the same actress.*

*All other parts played by members of the company, in particular
that marked* SINGER – *who can and will be played by multiple
people.*

Setting

The play is set in Berlin in 1981.

*This text went to press before the end of rehearsals and so may
differ slightly from the play as performed.*

Prologue

A little boy walks out on to stage. He is YOUNG WOYZECK.

He looks down on the floor.

He starts to chalk it out.

He continues this as the audience enter.

As he chalks it, things start to appear.

Around him and behind him.

And then a SINGER *appears behind him – with the house lights still up – and opens their mouth and starts to sing.*

And as they sing so things are built and transformed and grow.

SINGER.
    The sun had set behind yon hills,
    Across yon dreary moor,
    Weary and lame, a boy there came
    Up to a farmer's door
    'Can you tell me if any there be
    That will give me employ,
    To plough and sow, and reap and mow,
    And be a farmer's boy?

    My father is dead, and Mother is left
    With five children, great and small;
    And what is worse for Mother still,
    I'm the oldest of them all.
    Though little, I'll work as hard as a Turk,
    If you'll give me employ,
    To plough and sow, and reap and mow,
    And be a farmer's boy.

    And if that you won't me employ,
    One favour I've to ask, –
    Will you shelter me, till break of day,

> From this cold winter's blast?
> At break of day, I'll trudge away
> Elsewhere to seek employ,
> To plough and sow, and reap and mow,
> And be a farmer's – '

MOTHER. Frank.

YOUNG WOYZECK *runs offstage*.

ACT ONE

Scene One

A simple bedroom. MARIE *and* WOYZECK *lie barely dressed on the bed.* MARIE *is Irish and speaks with an Irish accent,* WOYZECK *is English and speaks with an English accent. Their German pronunciation is terrible, but it tries hard.*

WOYZECK. Ich liebe dich.

MARIE. Ick leeb dich.

He looks at her.

WOYZECK. Ich liebe dich.

MARIE. Ich liebe dich.

WOYZECK. I'll lick dick.

MARIE. I'll lick dick means…

WOYZECK. Drum roll.

MARIE *laughs.*

MARIE. Cos I'll like this?

WOYZECK. You will.

He looks at her.

Do the thing where you do the air drums.

MARIE. I'm not doing the fucking air drums – tell me what I'll lick dick means.

WOYZECK. I love you.

MARIE *laughs.*

MARIE. I'll lick dick means I love you?

WOYZECK. It's the reason why I love this language.

MARIE. Say it again.

WOYZECK. I'll lick dick.

MARIE. Say it properly.

WOYZECK. Ich liebe dich.

MARIE. Ich liebe dich.

WOYZECK. No. I'll lick your dick.

MARIE. No. I'll lick your dick. Tell me another.

WOYZECK. Ich will ficken.

MARIE. Ich will ficken. What does that mean?

WOYZECK. Guess.

MARIE. This is going to take ages if you're going to prick it
out on every single one. What does it mean?

WOYZECK. I want to fuck.

*She looks at him and then she kisses him and then she
hits him.*

MARIE. You're teaching me all the useful stuff, you know that?
I'm going to go to the greengrocer's and all I'm going to be
able to say is 'I love you' and 'I want to fuck'. And he'll say
'Okay love, but do you want carrots or sprouts with that?'

WOYZECK. Okay, I'll teach you something good.

MARIE. Thank you.

WOYZECK. Deine Oma masturbiert im stehen!

MARIE. That's about masturbation, isn't it?

WOYZECK. It might be.

MARIE. You're a dick.

WOYZECK. Do you want to know what it means?

MARIE. No, I want to know how to get the bus into town so
I can buy cabbage.

WOYZECK. It's a massive insult round here apparently.

MARIE. Go on then.

WOYZECK. Deine Oma masturbiert im stehen. I wish you'd
do your drums.

She does her air drums, they're magnificent.

Your grandmother masturbates standing up.

MARIE. What?

WOYZECK. Worst thing you can say to a guy – 'Oi, Franz, you
know your granny? She finger-fucks her fanny when she's
standing up.' I mean, of all the things, right?

He thinks it's funnier than she does.

MARIE. How do you ask for the bus timetable?

WOYZECK. I don't know, I haven't learnt that yet.

MARIE. You're useless.

He kisses her.

WOYZECK. Du bist 'ne Schlampe!

MARIE. Whatever you just said, if it's not 'You're beautiful'
then I'm going to –

WOYZECK. I said 'You're the only girl I've ever loved'.

He kisses her again, she kisses back.

MARIE. Did you? Really?

WOYZECK (*with a grin*). Well. It's what I wanted to say.

MARIE. And you actually said?

WOYZECK. I called you a slut – but to be really clear –

She hits him, outraged, but with a giggle.

I only learnt the dirty stuff. It's hard, learning new words.

MARIE. You're bad.

WOYZECK. You're beautiful.

MARIE. You're beautiful.

WOYZECK. You're more beautiful.

She crawls on top of him. She kisses him some more.

MARIE. What's I want to fuck again?

WOYZECK. Ich will ficken.

MARIE. Ich will ficken.

He kisses her back.

WOYZECK. Ich will ficken too.

MARIE *laughs. He flips her on to her back, they begin to get in to it, then there's the sound of a baby crying.*

They both stop. They lie back on the bed.

You think she's got a timer thing, just as we – you know – she goes – 'Mummy don't fuck Daddy'?

MARIE. No.

WOYZECK. No?

MARIE. No.

WOYZECK. When was the last time she fed?

MARIE. About an hour ago.

WOYZECK. So she's probably just shit herself then.

MARIE. You want me to go?

WOYZECK. No. I'll go.

He gets out of bed. He turns around to her. He begins to dress in full military uniform.

This place – it doesn't need to be scary.

MARIE. I'm not scared.

WOYZECK. We're going to be fine.

MARIE. I know.

WOYZECK. I'll get the money together.

MARIE. I know you will.

WOYZECK. I hate you being here.

MARIE. I love being with you.

WOYZECK. Fuck I'm lucky.

MARIE. Yeah. You are.

*He walks out towards the baby's cries. And then he stops
again and he looks back at her.*

WOYZECK. Sometimes I get...

MARIE. If you're not going to go, I need to.

WOYZECK. No, I know, I just... Sometimes I feel too lucky,
you know. Like that something will – something is too good.

MARIE. We're fine.

WOYZECK. I'll lick dick.

MARIE. I'll lick dick too.

WOYZECK *smiles and then exits.*

Scene Two

It's hot. WOYZECK *and* ANDREWS *are standing in full
military uniform. They're sweating. They're on patrol at
a checkpoint.*

WOYZECK. And if we see anyone?

ANDREWS. Point your gun, and then take a photo.

WOYZECK. That's what we're supposed to do?

ANDREWS. That's what they said we're supposed to do.

WOYZECK. And if they shoot us when we're taking a photo?

ANDREWS. They won't. Probably.

WOYZECK. Point your gun. Take a photo. And if they keep
coming.

ANDREWS. Then issue a warning.

WOYZECK. And then...

ANDREWS. ...Then you can shoot them.

WOYZECK. Good job the border is so fucking big.

ANDREWS *laughs*.

ANDREWS. The humble camera. The best way to protect against the Communist rampage.

He shouts across the border.

Ivans can't afford them, you see.

WOYZECK *looks around*.

WOYZECK. It's hot.

ANDREWS. I've been hotter.

WOYZECK. When?

ANDREWS. Exercise in Sierra Leone. When they thought they were preparing us for engagement in Afghanistan. Even my socks smelt of ball sweat.

WOYZECK *nods. He walks up and down.*

WOYZECK. I keep having these dreams. About Marie.

ANDREWS. I have dreams about your Marie too.

WOYZECK. It starts and she's just standing there and we're surrounded.

ANDREWS. Okay.

WOYZECK. And this man says – one of the men surrounding us –

ANDREWS. Mostly men, is it?

WOYZECK. – for every item of clothing she takes off I'm going to hurt you. He says. To me.

ANDREWS. What does he look like? The man?

WOYZECK. He's wearing a mask.

ANDREWS. This sounds like one of your best dreams.

WOYZECK. He hits me with a rubber-headed mallet – just lightly at first and then harder – on the outside of my thighs, outside of my arms, my arse – for the first layers – socks – earrings – her scarf –

ANDREWS. She sounds well dressed.

WOYZECK. As it gets down to her jumper and then her dress and slip – he takes the rubber head off to reveal a steel hammer underneath. And starts hitting my knees, my elbows, the underside of my feet – and then when she's in her underwear – he takes the steel hammer head off to reveal this sort of blade – which he repeatedly smashes into my ribs as she stands there naked. What do you think that means?

ANDREWS *looks at him.*

ANDREWS. You wake up with a hard-on?

WOYZECK. No.

ANDREWS. Then you're fine.

WOYZECK. Yeah?

ANDREWS *laughs.*

ANDREWS. The twisted way your mind works.

WOYZECK. It's not that twisted. What's a hard-on got to do with it?

ANDREWS. Pain, mate. It's whether you enjoy pain or not.

He suddenly lowers his gun. WOYZECK *turns and does the same.*

WOYZECK. What?

ANDREWS. Thought I saw something.

He stares at the gates.

You should have got a stiffy, after that dream. I got a stiffy just listening to you have that dream.

He ranges his gun around.

I once had a dream that I accidentally shot my knob off, I woke up and I had a stiffy. Though I think that was more of a reassurance thing.

He lowers his gun. He takes out a camera and takes a picture of the gates.

It was nothing.

WOYZECK *stares at the spot a bit longer.*

Missed a good one last night.

WOYZECK. Did I?

ANDREWS. Everyone was out.

WOYZECK. I was with Marie.

ANDREWS. Started in The Lion and Unicorn but then we went out, sampled the local life.

WOYZECK. Good?

ANDREWS. Say what you like about the Germans – they know how to brew a lager and they know how to breed a lass.

WOYZECK. You met someone?

ANDREWS. Nice girl, great arse, bit worried she had hairy pits and no way to check – but I'm like, fuck it, you'll do – we're snogging – I've got my hand in her knickers, she's got her hand in my cacks. Then this big woman – like eighteen stone – approaches behind me and says something…

WOYZECK. What?

ANDREWS. Fuck knows. She was talking in German. The two hammer off against each other. No idea what they're saying but they're saying. Anyway, then the one I'd been snogging, said – I should come with the pair of them.

WOYZECK. Pair of them? The eighteen-stone one too –

ANDREWS. Hey, kid. If you haven't wrestled a big bird, you haven't lived. Took me back to their apartment, showed me things I didn't think I'd ever see.

WOYZECK. You're a romantic.

ANDREWS *laughs.*

ANDREWS. I feel soiled. But good soiled.

You did the solid thing, my friend, bring the nice Irish pussy with you. Clean. Good. Shaved in all the right places, hairy in all the wrong. But if you ever get bored of Marie – these German girls are worth a sample.

WOYZECK. I won't get bored of Marie.

ANDREWS. No.

WOYZECK. She might – get bored of me.

ANDREWS. Like fuck.

WOYZECK. The flat's not great.

ANDREWS. Above an abattoir, I'm guessing not?

WOYZECK. It's not an abattoir – it's a place where they kill meat in a halal way.

ANDREWS. A halal abattoir?

WOYZECK. We can hear them – sometimes – the sounds the animals make. And we can smell the shit and the meat – when the weather is hot. I see her looking – thinking 'Why doesn't he do better.' Fuck, I need money.

ANDREWS. Get a loan.

WOYZECK. From who? From what? I'm overdrawn already. Her family? No. The army? No.

ANDREWS. A mate.

WOYZECK. Can you lend me three hundred quid please?

ANDREWS. You see? That's a start.

WOYZECK. Can you?

ANDREWS. Wish I could. Spent it all last night on lager and lubrication.

WOYZECK *nods and smiles*.

WOYZECK. Fuck, it's hot.

ANDREWS. It is, isn't it?

Scene Three

Captain's quarters.

WOYZECK *is shaving* CAPTAIN THOMPSON. *There's a fan beating overhead.*

CAPTAIN THOMPSON. Has anyone ever told you that you have soft hands?

WOYZECK. No, sir.

CAPTAIN THOMPSON. Good, because they'd be lying. The chin is the second most vulnerable part of the body after the ballsack, be gentle with it.

WOYZECK (*laugh*). Sorry, sir.

CAPTAIN THOMPSON. Slowly, boy, be gentle, be slow, our tour's only just begun – you're out here for a good while yet –

WOYZECK. Yes, sir.

The CAPTAIN *adjusts his mirror so as to look at* WOYZECK.

CAPTAIN THOMPSON. Woyzeck, you look hunted. Please tell me it's not because I insulted your shaving skills.

WOYZECK. No, sir. But I'm not hunted.

CAPTAIN THOMPSON. Is that right? Well, I'm not one to interfere. Maybe it's haunted. Hunted or haunted. The Captain's dilemma. The whole British army looks haunted, haunted is nothing to worry about, but hunted... Haunted men just cry. We all cry. But a hunted man. A hunted man is a man who'll do something. And you never want a soldier who does something, you understand? Fucks with obedience.

He looks at WOYZECK *carefully.*

They think – they've enquired whether you need some counselling – for what happened out there...

WOYZECK. I don't, sir.

CAPTAIN THOMPSON. Orphan, right? You're an orphan. Bought up in an orphanage.

WOYZECK. Not quite, sir.

CAPTAIN THOMPSON. No shame in needing help. Especially
  if it'll help you look less hunted. We don't want you twisted
  like Oliver, do we?

WOYZECK. I'm not hunted.

CAPTAIN THOMPSON. Maybe you think I don't give a fuck?
  Maybe I don't? But I do want you to be a decent soldier and
  not to get my balls in a tangle. And I'm not sure you're not a
  ball-tangler.

WOYZECK. The thing is, sir, if you're asking, I am short of –
  a little short of – money –

CAPTAIN THOMPSON. Don't believe what they say about
  Germany – this isn't a doss house – this isn't a place where
  nothing happens – we've plenty to fear – the Soviets are
  looking to take advantage of our situation – they know
  Northern Ireland has distracted us – and our work here – it
  matters. First line of defence.

WOYZECK. Yes, sir.

CAPTAIN THOMPSON. The locals are benign I would say –
  don't like our low-flying jets but mostly benign – but around
  every corner is a Stasi sympathiser – or Stasi spy – and that
  means – caution, always caution.

WOYZECK. Yes, sir.

CAPTAIN THOMPSON. I'm telling you I need you to be a
  decent soldier.

WOYZECK. I am decent.

CAPTAIN THOMPSON. The trouble is, an indecent man would
  give indecent word to that question, wouldn't they? I worry
  about you, Woyzeck.

WOYZECK. Yes, sir. Sorry, sir.

CAPTAIN THOMPSON. Bringing up money like that, it's
  vulgar.

WOYZECK. I thought you hadn't heard me, sir.

CAPTAIN THOMPSON. Tell me – what's the weather like
  today, Woyzeck?

WOYZECK. There's a fierce wind, sir. You think that means something?

CAPTAIN THOMPSON. I think that means there's a fierce wind. I suppose it must be north-southerly.

WOYZECK. Yes, sir.

CAPTAIN THOMPSON. Got you! North-southerly Woyzeck. Listen to the words, north-southerly. What the fuck is north-southerly? Why the fuck would that exist?

WOYZECK. I was just agreeing with what you said, sir. I just hadn't heard of it – north-southerly – so was just agreeing with what you said.

CAPTAIN THOMPSON. Your hand is shaking, I'm not sure it'll help you shave me, do you?

WOYZECK. Sorry, sir.

He puts down the blade and then picks up the blade and starts shaving the CAPTAIN *again.*

CAPTAIN THOMPSON. Do you know why I chose you for this task?

WOYZECK. No.

CAPTAIN THOMPSON. I wanted to tell the other men – this is my man – I know what happened in Belfast and I wanted to say – this is my man.

WOYZECK. Thank you, sir.

CAPTAIN THOMPSON. Quis Separabit.

WOYZECK. Yes.

CAPTAIN THOMPSON. Your Dragoon motto. Woyzeck. Who shall separate us.

WOYZECK. I know, sir.

CAPTAIN THOMPSON. And who shall, Woyzeck? Who shall? You remain my man but you have to buck up a little bit. Think. Obedience is not blind. It requires intelligence.

WOYZECK. I love my job, sir. I love being part of the British army, sir. It's the greatest army in the world, sir.

CAPTAIN THOMPSON. It certainly is.

There's a silence.

Ich stimme dir vollkommen zu. I totally agree with you.

WOYZECK. Ich stimme dir vollkommen zu.

CAPTAIN THOMPSON. Latin to German in one wonderful leap. Now how can we help you remember that? Strim my welcome mat. Does that work? It does. Bit of fun.

WOYZECK. North-southerly. I should have. I'm sorry I didn't understand what you were testing me for.

CAPTAIN THOMPSON. The best tests are not announced. You had your mind on other things. That won't be the case any more.

WOYZECK. No, sir.

CAPTAIN THOMPSON. Clear your mind of all but the most essential things. That's what I do.

WOYZECK. Yes, sir. Thank you, sir. Sometimes though, sir – my mind doesn't stay – doesn't stay clear.

CAPTAIN THOMPSON. If it was easy everyone would do it.

WOYZECK. One thing. One thing on my mind. Sir. Is money though, sir. Do you think? Are there any ways to earn some money?

CAPTAIN THOMPSON. You get paid, Woyzeck.

WOYZECK. Some extra money.

CAPTAIN THOMPSON. You get paid, Woyzeck.

WOYZECK. Yes, sir.

CAPTAIN THOMPSON. And if you haven't enough – well, then make that enough be enough, that's my advice. Vulgar advice for a vulgar question.

He goes back to shaving. CAPTAIN THOMPSON *laughs.*

North-southerly.

WOYZECK. Yes, sir. Sorry, sir.

Scene Four

The flat.

MAGGIE *is well put together, she looks around the flat suspiciously.*

MAGGIE. It's a thing we do – wives of the officers – pay little visits – where we can – I bought scones.

MARIE. Oh. Lovely.

MAGGIE. I didn't bake them. I do bake but not well. Spare you that at least. But one of the other girls does bake. Obsequious little thing. So I suppose you'd call this a regift. She baked them for me, I bring them to you.

MARIE. Thank you.

MAGGIE. Trying to diet actually, so you're doing me the favour. Thinking of starting an aerobics class at the wives' club, would you come?

MARIE. I don't know.

MAGGIE. What's that smell?

MARIE. Butcher's. Downstairs.

MAGGIE. Gosh. Really? How extraordinary.

MARIE. Yes.

MAGGIE. You know, I thought for a moment, the smell might be the baby. I thought – that's one way to put your foot in it – foot and a leg – what's that smell? Oh, it's the baby.

MARIE. She does smell.

MAGGIE. Oh, they do, they do, I've three. Awful smells, all three of them. But this smell is quite pungent, so I'm relieved it's not your baby.

MARIE. Yes.

MAGGIE. Catholic, am I right?

MARIE. You are.

MAGGIE. That's sort of mostly why I'm here, in fact – bit of an introduction, though the husbands do frown when you're on the side so to speak – which you are – and there's nothing wrong with that – but I thought I could recruit you. We're on a bit of a fundraising drive.

MARIE. We don't have any money.

MAGGIE. Oh darling, that much is clear – one does wonder if this is the best he could do – but no, not looking for that – how's your German –

She produces from her bag a set of little envelopes.

Well, not to worry, whatever it is, they know why you're there if you have these. The thing is I'm rushed off my feet with this entertainment position I've taken on – so much cheese – so much wine. Too much cheese frankly, and it's very hard to source out here. So I wondered if you could help.

MARIE. If I can…

MAGGIE. I knew it. I knew you could. Strong Irish stock. Look at those legs. My grandmother was Irish as it happens. Ran off and joined the circus and met my grandfather – who owned the circus. That's the way lives change, isn't it? Extraordinary man. The circus went bust but he ended up making all his money in washing detergent.

MARIE. What do you want me to do?

MAGGIE starts producing set after set of envelopes.

MAGGIE. Two thousand little envelopes. You post them through the door and then you knock on the door seven days later and you say – 'Hello, did you manage to put money in the envelopes' – in German. I forget the German for it. Actually, they mostly understand English. And Catholicism is very popular here.

MARIE. Two thousand seems a lot.

MAGGIE. It is a lot. And here are – the route plans to go with them. It's a wonderful way to get to know the neighbourhood. And so easy with a pram.

MARIE. We don't have a pram.

MAGGIE. Well, he should do something about that quick-smart. You need a pram.

MARIE. Can you help? Can you help us?

MAGGIE. Oh, I'm sorry.

She thinks. She thinks.

I'm sorry. I'm afraid that's a matter for the husbands. I used to get involved. I do like to get involved. But I found that I never helped, and no one wants to be in the way. It doesn't help anything. But he should talk to someone. And get some money flowing in here.

She waits a moment.

I need your word you will deliver the envelopes.

MARIE. I'll deliver your envelopes.

MAGGIE. We had one girl who threw them away. That was quite a storm, I can tell you.

Suddenly WOYZECK *and* ANDREWS *appear.*

ANDREWS (*sings*).
     Two hares sitting there
     Eating the grass
     Until it was bare –
     Eating up the tiny shoots,
     Eating the grass
     Down to the roots –

MAGGIE. Ah. Hello.

WOYZECK. Ah, I didn't know we had –

MAGGIE. This is him, is it?

MARIE. Yes, this is Frank.

MAGGIE. And who's this with him?

ANDREWS. Andrews, ma'am.

MAGGIE. Have we met, Andrews?

ANDREWS. Just a familiar face I think, ma'am.

MAGGIE. Or I've been watching you and not telling you of it.

ANDREWS *grins*.

WOYZECK. We're just off to The Lion and Unicorn. We wondered if –

MAGGIE. Wasting your money on drinking? And are you wearing your arms?

ANDREWS. Got to check these in first.

MAGGIE. You bought your guns into a civilian house?

ANDREWS. Not for – we was just walking past –

MAGGIE. I could get you in considerable trouble, soldier.

ANDREWS. You could, ma'am.

MAGGIE. Tell you what, let me touch it and we'll say no more about it.

ANDREWS. Been waiting for you to ask, ma'am.

MAGGIE *walks over to* ANDREWS, *she touches his gun, he slaps her arse*.

MAGGIE. Soldiers.

She walks out with a laugh.

ANDREWS *looks after her. He mouths 'Married?' at* MARIE – *she nods*.

ANDREWS *follows* MAGGIE *out*.

WOYZECK *approaches* MARIE *awkwardly*.

WOYZECK. Who was she?

MARIE. Two different people I think.

WOYZECK. How are you?

MARIE. What's wrong with you? Coming in like that.

WOYZECK. She didn't like me.

MARIE. She told me I should expect more of you. I told her that I understood. What you were.

WOYZECK. What am I?

MARIE. I haven't completely decided yet but I know it's bad.

She laughs and leans up and kisses him and then looks at the baby.

WOYZECK. Is he okay?

MARIE. Fine. Sticking to the schedule.

WOYZECK *leans over the child.*

WOYZECK. He's sweating.

MARIE. It's hot. All I can smell is meat on me. Do I smell of meat? Does she? All she can smell is meat. The slighty sick smell of meat stewing.

She sings to the baby.

> If you don't close the window tight
> The gypsy boy will come at night
> And he will take you by the hand
> And lead you off to gypsy land.

WOYZECK. That's a strange rhyme.

MARIE. Something my mother used to sing me.

WOYZECK. Who sung it her?

MARIE *just looks at him,* WOYZECK *looks over into the crib.*

Look at him. He's hot. He's sweating.

MARIE. He's okay. I'd rather he be hot than cold.

WOYZECK. We even sweat in our sleep. Us Woyzecks.

MARIE. That's a bit of you, is it? That's your bit, the sweating?

WOYZECK. Yes.

MARIE. Well, good. Good that that's what you bring. I give our son my beautiful eyes and fine chin and you give him an ability to sweat a lot.

WOYZECK. And his farting. I'll also take responsibility for his terrible wind.

MARIE. Not to mention the terrible roof you place above his head.

WOYZECK. Also responsible for that, yes.

He kisses her, she kisses him back.

MARIE. You've ruined his mother and you've ruined him.

She kisses him again.

Scene Five

A surgery.

WOYZECK *has his top off – he's being examined.*

DOCTOR MARTENS. You're in good shape.

WOYZECK. Thank you.

DOCTOR MARTENS. No, you are, you're handsome.

WOYZECK. Thank you.

DOCTOR MARTENS. And you have big shoulders.

WOYZECK. Okay.

DOCTOR MARTENS. You're a big man.

WOYZECK. I try to keep in good condition.

DOCTOR MARTENS. You don't smoke.

WOYZECK. No.

DOCTOR MARTENS. Do you drink?

WOYZECK. Only a bit, sir.

DOCTOR MARTENS. Only a little. Why?

WOYZECK. I don't like what it does to my brain.

DOCTOR MARTENS. What does it do to your brain?

WOYZECK. It makes me less like myself, sir.

DOCTOR MARTENS. I'm not one of your knights, Mr Woyzeck – you don't need to 'sir' me.

WOYZECK. Okay.

DOCTOR MARTENS. Did your father drink? Your mother? I'm interested what convinced you – a young man – to stop drinking?

WOYZECK. I didn't know my father or mother.

DOCTOR MARTENS. You're an orphan?

WOYZECK. Yes.

DOCTOR MARTENS. Interesting. And why wouldn't an orphan drink then? What convinced you to not drink?

WOYZECK. I don't know, sir. I just don't like it.

DOCTOR MARTENS. You fear yourself when drunk?

WOYZECK. No, sir. Sorry, no.

DOCTOR MARTENS. You're nervous.

WOYZECK. I want to pass the test.

DOCTOR MARTENS. What test?

WOYZECK. The one that says I can go on your trial.

DOCTOR MARTENS. So you're giving me the answers I want rather than the ones I need.

WOYZECK. No.

DOCTOR MARTENS. Because I need the truth.

WOYZECK. I'm telling the truth.

DOCTOR MARTENS. It sounds like you're twisting your truth in order to please me, in order to pass my test.

WOYZECK. No, sir.

DOCTOR MARTENS. Why do you want to be on my trial?

WOYZECK. Because I need the money.

DOCTOR MARTENS. Why do you need the money?

WOYZECK. Because I've got a baby.

DOCTOR MARTENS. Babies don't cost money. They drink their mother's milk.

WOYZECK. Nappies and...

DOCTOR MARTENS. Wash their nappies.

WOYZECK. Somewhere for her to sleep.

DOCTOR MARTENS. Build a box. I'm being facetious. Ignore me. I like to joke. Though I am fascinated why you don't drink more. Most soldiers drink, and you are a soldier, am I correct?

WOYZECK *hesitates*.

WOYZECK. Yes.

DOCTOR MARTENS. Do you have permission from your commanding officers to do my study?

WOYZECK. No.

DOCTOR MARTENS. Good. So now we understand why you're nervous. It's not because you wanted to be chosen for my study, it's because you were frightened that I'd discover you were a soldier and a liar.

WOYZECK *looks at the* DOCTOR.

WOYZECK. I need the money.

DOCTOR MARTENS. In order to find somewhere for your baby that is not a box.

WOYZECK. I thought I could sell my blood, but when I asked them they said the best way to make money here was to talk to you.

DOCTOR MARTENS. I've never had a soldier on a study of mine before. Not a German. Not an English. Not even an American.

WOYZECK. I won't tell them if you won't.

DOCTOR MARTENS. You won't tell your army doctors?

WOYZECK. No.

DOCTOR MARTENS *thinks*.

DOCTOR MARTENS. The occupation of Germany. A strange thing, don't you think?

WOYZECK. I don't think…

DOCTOR MARTENS. We are a richer country than you are, we have produced better science, arguably better art, we are thinner than you, this is medical fact you understand, and we are prettier than you, and yet we need you to control us because once we went a little bit mad. But you also went mad, the blood on the hands of the British Empire, that is a lot of blood… Don't you think?

WOYZECK. Yes.

DOCTOR MARTENS. But what I think makes it most fun of all – is that your occupation mostly consists of you guarding another country's nuclear weapons. That is what you do. The British. Guard the American's ability to kill Soviet Russia.

WOYZECK. Yes.

DOCTOR MARTENS. Would you agree with anything I said in order to be on my trial?

WOYZECK. I don't care for politics.

DOCTOR MARTENS. Is there nothing else you can do for money?

WOYZECK. No.

DOCTOR MARTENS. I am not sure my trial is a good one. Like you, I am paid. If you want to do it…

WOYZECK. I do.

The DOCTOR *looks at* WOYZECK *for a long time – and then makes a decision – he nods, he'll let* WOYZECK *take part.*

DOCTOR MARTENS. Read this and sign here.

WOYZECK *signs the piece of paper.*

Did you read it?

WOYZECK. No.

DOCTOR MARTENS. We're calling it Trial P. These may be – placebos. They may not. Do you know what a placebo is?

WOYZECK. What's it a trial of?

DOCTOR MARTENS. You do not need know. Come every Monday so we may study you. And take the pills. If you don't take the pills I'll know.

WOYZECK. I'll take the pills.

The DOCTOR *hands* WOYZECK *a glass of water.* WOYZECK *takes a green pill.*

Thanks. I won't let you down.

DOCTOR MARTENS. Always strange when people think to give that reassurance. It presumes I'm scared you will let me down. I'm not scared of that in the slightest.

Scene Six

The top of a multi-storey car park.

WOYZECK *is leading* MARIE. *Both are smiling.*

WOYZECK. I wanted you to see this.

MARIE. I don't understand what there is to see.

WOYZECK. Drink some more.

MARIE. I've drunk too much. Don't make me drink too much.

WOYZECK. You can handle it.

MARIE. There's a whole lot I can handle. Can we find a phone? I need to check on the baby...

WOYZECK. The baby has your milk. It has a roof. Andrews is looking after it. He looked after his sister's child. He knows what he's doing. Tonight has to be about the two of us.

MARIE. Does it?

WOYZECK. Not too much further.

MARIE. You're giddy.

WOYZECK. No. I'm not. I'm happy. I'm strong.

MARIE. Okay. Weirdo happy strong man.

She smiles at him weirdly, he doesn't smile back.

Honestly, I just wanted a nice meal and now I'm climbing some sort of –

WOYZECK. Multi-storey car park.

MARIE. Searching for what exactly?

WOYZECK. Do you mind if I put my hands over your eyes?

MARIE. Yes.

WOYZECK. We're almost too late to see it.

MARIE. What are we trying to see?

WOYZECK. I'm going to put my hands over your eyes whether you like it or not…

MARIE. You fucking try it.

WOYZECK *puts his hands around her waist, she runs from him, screeching, he chases after her…*

WOYZECK. Marie, Marie, be careful, be careful.

He grabs her again – and this time she can't get away.

We're six storeys up and you're running around like a kid.

MARIE. You're chasing me. You're wanting to blindfold me.

WOYZECK. I do.

MARIE. I'll scream.

WOYZECK. You won't.

MARIE. You're sure about that?

WOYZECK. I am.

MARIE. And what makes you so sure?

WOYZECK. Part of you likes it.

MARIE. Do I now?

WOYZECK. You do.

He kisses her.

Part of you likes being controlled by a big strong man.

MARIE. A man who won't even stretch to buying me an ice cream. Some fucking man.

But she says it with a laugh, and kisses him. He kisses her back and then with one arm still firmly around her waist, he moves his hand up – first to her breast which he squeezes –

Oi. You haven't earnt that.

And then over her face to cover her eyes.

Fuck off.

WOYZECK. I've got money.

MARIE. Frank…

WOYZECK. We can't move out yet but I've got money.

MARIE. How've you got money?

WOYZECK. Details. I'm going to carry you.

MARIE. I want to know how you've got money.

WOYZECK. Let me be the man, let me be the man on this one.

MARIE. I'm going to bite you.

WOYZECK. Stay calm and don't wriggle too much otherwise I might drop you off the top of a really tall building.

MARIE. Fuck you.

WOYZECK. I mean it. I want to be careful with you. It has to be this exact place. I think – if I'm right – it's almost time for –

MARIE. This better be worth it, Frank.

WOYZECK. Five, four, three, two, one.

He removes his hands. She looks around – an anticipatory smile on her face.

The smile fades slightly, in mild confusion.

MARIE. What am I looking at?

WOYZECK. The free world and the unfree. And in a moment, I timed it wrong, I couldn't look at my watch. In a moment all the lights will fire up.

MARIE. That's East Germany?

WOYZECK. That's where the Soviets are.

MARIE. The buildings are bigger than I thought they'd be.

WOYZECK. I know. I found that surprising too. Don't you think it's extraordinary – we're free and they're not. Even watching them makes me feel – lucky.

MARIE. Can you see any of them? Have you brought binoculars up here?

Suddenly the streetlights light.

Oh, that is...

WOYZECK. Isn't it? I always think of it like a spider – the way it all just sort of – the way it doesn't happen all at the same time – it sort of crawls.

He looks at MARIE.

I've bought you something.

He brings out a small box.

MARIE. But we've no money.

WOYZECK. I told you, I got money.

MARIE. But not for this.

WOYZECK. I needed to tell you I loved you.

She opens it, it's a simple and elegant necklace.

MARIE. It's beautiful.

He puts it around her neck.

They kiss.

They sit in silence together – happy.

WOYZECK. I never had someone to love before you. It feels like an extraordinary thing.

MARIE. That's a nice thing to say.

WOYZECK. Have I made your life better?

MARIE. What do you think they're doing over there?

WOYZECK. Eating. Sleeping. Shitting. Fucking.

MARIE. We could go over, for the day, Apparently cassettes cost much less over there.

WOYZECK. I don't want to go over there.

MARIE. Frightened you'll like it?

WOYZECK. No.

MARIE. You haven't made my life better, but I love our child very much.

WOYZECK. I need to have saved you.

MARIE. Why do you need to have saved me?

WOYZECK. I've saved you, Marie – you'll see.

MOTHER. Frankie. Frank.

MOTHER *enters the stage at the back.*

YOUNG WOYZECK *enters the stage.*

He draws around WOYZECK*'s shape on the floor.*

Frankie. Frank.

YOUNG WOYZECK *looks up at* WOYZECK. *Who doesn't look back.*

WOYZECK. I've saved her.

YOUNG WOYZECK *just stays, staring.*

No. I have.

Scene Seven

It's once again boiling hot – they're on patrol at a checkpoint.

WOYZECK. I'd shoot.

ANDREWS. You wouldn't.

WOYZECK. I would.

ANDREWS. Eight years old.

WOYZECK. If he was coming towards me and I believed he was dangerous.

ANDREWS. Seven years old.

WOYZECK. Yes.

ANDREWS. Six years old. If a six-year-old little comtot – little mick – if he was coming hard at you.

ANDREWS *looks at him.*

Hesitation.

WOYZECK. Maybe.

ANDREWS. Five.

WOYZECK. No.

ANDREWS *laughs.*

ANDREWS. There's your line.

WOYZECK. There's my line.

ANDREWS. Hesitation at six, definite no at five.

WOYZECK. I don't think a five-year-old is knowing what they're doing.

ANDREWS. But a six-year-old – he could.

WOYZECK. I knew what I was doing at that age.

ANDREWS. You're sure?

WOYZECK. Yes.

ANDREWS. Your memory is better than mine.

WOYZECK *looks at* ANDREWS.

WOYZECK. Your line?

ANDREWS. Ten. Wouldn't shoot a kid less than ten.

WOYZECK. What if he looked really old?

ANDREWS. If he looked old – not my fault. If he's smoking a fag. Drinking a pint. Not my fault. But ten – it's a solid number for a cut-off.

WOYZECK. What if he had massive hands?

ANDREWS *laughs*.

ANDREWS. What do massive hands have to do with it?

WOYZECK. He could have massive hands. There's something about kids with massive hands.

ANDREWS. If he had massive hands I'd shoot him. But only for you.

WOYZECK. Thanks.

WOYZECK *looks at* ANDREWS.

I would – you know – seven and up – I would.

ANDREWS. There's things to envy about that.

WOYZECK. I have a job to do. I have more people to protect.

ANDREWS. I envy that. Like I say. I mean, I know it's bollocks but I envy that...

WOYZECK *looks at* ANDREWS.

I don't blame you for what you did. Belfast. I don't blame you for anything.

They both wipe sweat from their faces.

If I was to ask a favour...

WOYZECK. What?

ANDREWS. I need use of your gaff. We need use of your gaff.

WOYZECK. You and the officer's wife?

ANDREWS. Me and the officer's wife.

WOYZECK. You can have it.

ANDREWS. Thank you. If I could pay you…

WOYZECK. She could pay me.

ANDREWS. Her husband would notice. Thank you.

WOYZECK. My pleasure. So you two –

ANDREWS. Yes. Yes. And she smells so fucking – even her pussy tastes of money.

WOYZECK. That's good.

ANDREWS. She's teaching me things.

WOYZECK. That's good.

They stand in silence a moment more.

But she is married.

ANDREWS. The best ones always are. Bit of a tradition for me actually. I'm known as the wife-snatcher.

WOYZECK. The wife-snatcher.

ANDREWS. Always more grateful.

WOYZECK. Are they?

ANDREWS. When their men are doing a tour elsewhere normally. When their men are in Belfast or whatever. The clue is – look for washing powder left in the window – Omo washing powder –

WOYZECK. Omo washing powder.

ANDREWS. On My Own.

And then ANDREWS'*s facial expression changes entirely.*

Woyzeck.

He indicates a man, GDR CITIZEN, *is looking at them from across the gate.*

Get to fuck.

He points his gun at the GDR CITIZEN. *He takes a picture.*

And then an EAST GERMAN SOLDIER *on the other side comes and starts pulling the* GDR CITIZEN *away.*

Mach deinen Job.

EAST GERMAN SOLDIER. Fuck you, Englishman.

ANDREWS. Fuck you.

WOYZECK. Deine Oma masturbiert im stehen.

The EAST GERMAN SOLDIER *turns around. He looks at* WOYZECK. *Outraged.*

And then he walks away, dragging the GDR CITIZEN *with him.*

ANDREWS. What did you say to him?

WOYZECK. The Captain taught it to me.

ANDREWS. What did you say?

WOYZECK. I told him that his grandma masturbates standing up.

ANDREWS *laughs.*

ANDREWS. Being on guard with you is the best fucking fun, you know that?

WOYZECK. It's a massive insult here.

ANDREWS. He didn't like it.

ANDREWS *looks at* WOYZECK.

WOYZECK. Omo washing powder. I won't forget.

Beat.

I had this talk with her – last night – about how I didn't want her to be great – I've no issue with great – I just wanted her to be good – I wanted her to feel like she did – she's done good things. I said I hoped she took after her mother because I think her mother does good things, you know? I think her mother mostly thinks good thoughts.

ANDREWS. Are you talking about talking to your baby?

WOYZECK. Yes.

ANDREWS. Are you okay, Woyzeck?

WOYZECK. Do you ever feel too lucky?

ANDREWS. No. I'm in the British fucking army, course I don't.

Scene Eight

The flat.

WOYZECK *is on his own.*

SINGER.
>Britons once did loyally declaim
>About the way we rul'd the waves
>Ev'ry Briton's song was just the same,
>When singing of our soldier braves.
>All the world had heard it
>Wonder'd why we sang,
>And some have learn'd the reason why
>But we're forgetting it,
>And we're letting it
>Fade away and gradually die,
>Fade away and gradually die.
>So when we say that England's master,
>Remember who has made her so.

WOYZECK sits down – he looks around himself.
ANDREWS and MAGGIE run across the stage.

MAGGIE. Do they call you grunts because you grunt?

ANDREWS. All of us.

MAGGIE. All of you grunt?

ANDREWS. Yup.

They kiss. And then she runs on, ANDREWS *looks back to*
WOYZECK, and then follows her.

SINGER.
> It's the Soldiers of the Queen, my lads
> Who've been my lads,
> Who're seen my lads,
> In the fight for England's glory, lads,
> When we've had to show them what we mean:
> And when we say we've always won,
> And when they ask us how it's done,
> We'll proudly point to ev'ry one
> Of England's soldiers of the Queen!
> It's the Queen!

WOYZECK picks up and takes a pill. He looks at it. He swallows it. MARIE emerges from behind him.

MARIE. Excuse me, can I interest you in supporting the Catholic Church?

A donation envelope descends down from the ceiling. She knocks on another door.

Excuse me, would you be interested in supporting the Catholic Church?

WOYZECK takes another pill.

SINGER.
> War clouds gather over ev'ry land,
> Our flag is threaten'd east and west.
> Nations that we've shaken by the hand
> Our bold resources try to test
> They thought they found us sleeping
> Thought us unprepar'd.

There are the sound of shots from off. WOYZECK doesn't flinch, instead he takes another pill.

Another donation envelope falls, and then another.

LANDLORD. Money.

WOYZECK. Sorry?

LANDLORD. Money?

WOYZECK. No, I've paid, I remember paying...

LANDLORD. Your baby ruined the carpets.

WOYZECK. No, she didn't.

LANDLORD. I need money for that and a security deposit that she doesn't do it again.

WOYZECK. Everything smells of meat.

LANDLORD. And that's why it's cheap. I need money.

SINGER.
Because we have our party wars,
But Englishmen unite when they're call'd to fight
The battle for Old England's common cause,
The battle for Old England's common cause.
So when we say that England's master,
Remember who has made her so.

A baby starts crying, off. WOYZECK *looks towards it. He feels slightly dazed. He doesn't go to it. He takes another pill. The baby's screams get louder.*

WOYZECK. Please don't shit everywhere. Please don't.

SINGER.
It's the Soldiers of the Queen, my lads,
Who've been my lads,
Who're seen my lads,
In the fight for England's glory, lads,
When we have to show them what we mean:
And when we sat we've always won,
And when they ask us how it's done,
We'll proudly point to ev'ry one
Of England's soldiers of the Queen!
It's the Queen!

MARIE. Excuse me, can I interest you in supporting the Catholic Church?

WOYZECK *takes another pill and leaves the flat. The baby's screams get louder still.*

Twenty donation envelopes fall from the ceiling.

SINGER.
> Now we're rous'd we've buckled on our swords,
> We've done with diplomatic lingo,
> We'll do deeds to follow on our words,
> We'll show we're something more than 'jingo'.
> And though Old England's laws do not her sons compel
> To military duties do,
> We'll play them at their game, and show them all the same,
> An Englishman can be a soldier too,
> An Englishman can be a soldier too.
> So when we say that England's master,
> Remember who has made her so.

There are a volley of shots and then nothing.

WOYZECK. I've come for my money.

DOCTOR MARTENS. What?

WOYZECK. I keep taking the pills.

He shows him the bottle.

I've kept taking the pills.

DOCTOR MARTENS. No, you get your money at the start of the trial and then at the end.

WOYZECK. So when do I get paid again?

DOCTOR MARTENS. This was all written down. You should have read your contract.

WOYZECK. Can I do another trial?

DOCTOR MARTENS. Not whilst you're doing this one. You are still taking the pills?

WOYZECK. Yes.

DOCTOR MARTENS. What's going on with your eyes? Your pupils?

WOYZECK. What if I took the pills more quickly – could I do the trial quicker?

DOCTOR MARTENS. Of course you can't.

WOYZECK. I'm fine. This is fine. I'm fine.

He looks back, he sees his MOTHER. *She walks slowly towards him.*

I'm fine.

ACT TWO

The flat.

WOYZECK *sits in the dark. Somehow he seems beneath everything. He has a gun at his feet.*

MOTHER. Woyzeck.

She shouts again.

Woyzeck.

CAPTAIN THOMPSON. Woyzeck.

ANDREWS. Where the fuck are you? Woyzeck.

DOCTOR MARTENS. Woyzeck.

MOTHER. Woyzeck.

CAPTAIN THOMPSON. Woyzeck.

MOTHER. WOYZECK.

CAPTAIN THOMPSON. WOYZECK.

DOCTOR MARTENS. WOYZECK.

The light turns on. WOYZECK *wants to scream but he doesn't.*

MARIE *enters, she has the baby, she brings it in.*

She carefully puts the baby down.

MARIE. Fell asleep on me as I was delivering.

WOYZECK *says nothing.*

What are you sitting in the dark for?

WOYZECK. I didn't notice.

MARIE. Cat, are you? See in the dark, could you?

WOYZECK *takes a breath*.

WOYZECK. I think I'd be a good cat.

MARIE. You'd be a pretty good cat.

WOYZECK. Would you be a dog or a mouse – if I was a cat.

MARIE. What?

WOYZECK. Would you chase me or would I chase you?

MARIE. Fuck that, I'd be a tiger.

WOYZECK *takes a deep breath*.

Have you heard the news? They tried to kill the Pope.

WOYZECK. Yeah?

MARIE. It was in the papers.

WOYZECK. Yeah?

MARIE. Doesn't that scare you? His Holiness.

WOYZECK. Yeah.

MARIE. I'm not much of a Catholic any more but I would say –

WOYZECK. Yeah.

MARIE. If I was home right now, if I was home…

He walks away from her, he rubs his temples.

WOYZECK. You're not home. You're here.

MARIE *looks after him, she frowns*.

MARIE. You okay?

WOYZECK. Yeah.

MARIE. Why don't I believe that?

WOYZECK. I don't know. I'm okay.

MARIE. You're sweating.

WOYZECK. I always sweat. It's hot. It's the meat.

MARIE. You want to go lie down?

WOYZECK. No.

MARIE. You probably should.

WOYZECK. I probably shouldn't. If I sleep, I'm not sure I'll wake up. Besides, the Pope's been shot, probably no one should sleep.

MARIE *nods*.

MARIE. Landlord tried to catch me as I walked up the stairs.

WOYZECK. Yeah?

MARIE. Said you owed him.

WOYZECK. Yes.

MARIE. Looked at my arse again.

WOYZECK. Did he?

MARIE. And not in a subtle way.

WOYZECK. Yeah?

MARIE. One of those men who doesn't think he needs to hide it. Not that – I sometimes prefer those men if I'm honest. Those that don't hide it.

WOYZECK. Yeah?

MARIE. Anyway, the way he looks at me I should probably blow him once a month and we'd get this place rent free.

WOYZECK. Please don't.

MARIE. I was joking.

WOYZECK. Yeah. Don't joke about that.

MARIE. Okay, twitchy. I won't. But don't be – no need to be a cunt about it.

She laughs.

WOYZECK. She asleep?

MARIE. Yes.

WOYZECK. How long has she been down? She needs her sleep.

MARIE. I know.

WOYZECK. How long since her last feed?

MARIE. I didn't write it down. Are you sure you're okay?

WOYZECK *nods*.

MARIE *sees his gun*.

What's that doing here?

WOYZECK. It's got no ammunition in it.

MARIE. I thought you weren't supposed to have it out without being on patrol.

WOYZECK. I didn't check it back in. I'm pretending I lost it.

MARIE. Why would you do that?

WOYZECK. I'm selling it.

MARIE. You can't sell your gun.

WOYZECK. Why not?

MARIE. Because they'll send you to jail.

WOYZECK. No, they won't.

MARIE. Yes, they will.

WOYZECK. The Captain likes me.

MARIE. Doesn't stop him sending you to jail for selling your gun.

WOYZECK. I'll tell them I lost it.

MARIE. He won't believe you. I thought you'd got money.

WOYZECK. It wasn't enough.

MARIE. Frank…

WOYZECK. I keep offering to do things for people for money and they keep saying no and so I – need to think more – deeply.

MARIE. Selling a gun isn't thinking deeply. It's a thick idea.

WOYZECK. Don't call me thick. Don't do that.

MARIE. I was saying your idea was thick, and it is.

WOYZECK. I don't call you a whore, don't call me thick.

MARIE. I'm not a fucking whore.

He looms up over her.

WOYZECK. Offering people blowjobs.

MARIE. I was fucking joking.

WOYZECK. Offering people blowjobs.

MARIE. Okay. You're scaring me now.

WOYZECK. You dare. You dare fucking call me thick. You dare call me thick. You dare do that.

MARIE. You'll wake the baby.

WOYZECK. You'll wake the baby. You called me thick.

MARIE. I take it back.

He towers over her.

I take it back. You're scaring me. I take it back. Frank.

WOYZECK *looks at her.*

WOYZECK. I hate the way you say my name.

He steps back.

MARIE. Jesus.

WOYZECK *walks away.*

You looked like you wanted to bite me. Tear me apart. Jesus.

WOYZECK. I'm allowed to be angry.

MARIE. You're not allowed to hit me, you know that, right?

WOYZECK. I wasn't going to –

MARIE. My da hit my ma –

WOYZECK. I wasn't going to –

MARIE. I won't let it happen.

WOYZECK. I wouldn't hit you, I wouldn't do that.

MARIE *looks at him.*

You're safe with me.

MARIE *looks at him.*

My mother got beaten too. You're safe with me.

MARIE. I didn't know that.

WOYZECK. I wouldn't hit you.

MARIE. Who beat her?

WOYZECK. Whoever paid.

MARIE *frowns and nods.*

Do you remember the first moment when we met?

MARIE. Yes. In the pub.

WOYZECK. No. Not that – not the – first meeting – not do you remember the first meeting – do you remember the moment when we first saw each other? I don't mean the first words we spoke. I mean, the moment – the exact moment when we first met, when our eyes met.

MARIE. I don't think I remember the exact moment…

WOYZECK. I can still remember when I first saw you – as clearly as if it was yesterday.

MARIE. You really chose me for my personality then?

WOYZECK. No… I just…

MARIE. The thing about love at first sight is it's basically about wanting to bang someone, which is fine. I mean, absolutely fine. It's just – you know – I thought I was a bit more than a pair of tits and an arse, you know?

WOYZECK. I could see the person you were.

MARIE. Could you now?

WOYZECK. I could. And I couldn't hit you. Sorry for making you feel like that. Feeling like I could.

MARIE. Don't dwell on it.

WOYZECK. I can even describe exactly what you were wearing – you were in that blue dress –

MARIE. Okay. I'm not going to remember –

WOYZECK. Your white heels.

MARIE. You could be saying anything.

WOYZECK. And plain black tights. I remember, because a lot of the other women were wearing fish-nets.

MARIE. Fish-nets leave me cold on the way home.

WOYZECK. You had blue eye shadow, you had pale-pink lipstick – you had –

MARIE. You're sounding less like a lay and more like a stalker.

WOYZECK. And you had this smile, when you were talking to your friends, and then this laugh – your laugh sounded like the finest thing I ever heard. Not – it wasn't loud – it wasn't showing off or anything like that – it just sounded like it had joy in it.

MARIE *looks at him.*

MARIE. I'm not sure what's going on, but – you know what – I'm going to leave you be, go on another walk.

WOYZECK. I've scared you.

MARIE. I'll get over it, just – keep an eye on the baby – would you? Give me time for a stroll about, deliver some more of these fucking envelopes.

WOYZECK. I was trying to tell you I loved you and I scared you.

MARIE. You're always telling me you love me.

WOYZECK. And you don't like that?

MARIE. I'm not saying that. I'm just saying – well, it'd be nice to have a normal conversation every now and again, don't you think?

WOYZECK. What do you want to talk about? Should I ask you to marry me again?

MARIE. No. No. I said it's too soon for that. So…

WOYZECK. We'd get better accommodation. I wouldn't mind. I'd like it. I love you.

MARIE. Frank, I'm going to go out now.

WOYZECK. I can't think normal thoughts when I'm around you. I can't have a normal conversation.

MARIE. Because you're consumed by love?

WOYZECK. You don't like that?

MARIE. I just want you to be fifty per cent more fucking normal, okay?

WOYZECK. I'm trying really hard to build a life for us here.

MARIE. So the fuck am I!

WOYZECK. You should be grateful – you should be grateful – I'm climbing up mountains of shit – you should be grateful –

MARIE. Thanks for this meat palace. It's fucking lovely.

WOYZECK. Fuck!

MARIE. I'm going out, okay? I'm going out.

WOYZECK. Fuck!

He slams his head into the wall.

MARIE. Fuck.

He slams his head into the wall again.

Frank. Fuck, don't do that?

WOYZECK. I haven't hurt myself. Look. I'm fine.

MARIE. What the shit?

WOYZECK. I can walk in a straight line. Watch me walk in a straight line.

MARIE. I just watched you slam your head into a wall.

WOYZECK. I was showing you that I couldn't do you harm. I was showing you that I was sorry.

MARIE. That's a pretty strange thing to –

WOYZECK. And I need you to stay. Will you stay?

MARIE *looks at him.*

Can I look at her? Looking at her always makes me feel better.

He walks around and looks into the crib.

I am not a man – who'd ever hurt.

MARIE. You said.

WOYZECK. You don't believe it.

MARIE. If I say no – will you slam your head into a wall again?

WOYZECK. No. I'll just be disappointed.

MARIE. I don't understand you any more.

WOYZECK. I don't know why. I'm really easy to understand.

WOYZECK *leans in to the crib.*

Look at her. She's got the best of the world inside her, don't you think?

MARIE. She's got a mountain of shit. She's burning through those nappies.

WOYZECK. It's surprising – to me – how much of her I can see. She has so much of you inside her.

MARIE. She has your nose.

WOYZECK. Your eyes.

MARIE. Your smile.

WOYZECK. Your grace.

MARIE *melts slightly despite herself.*

MARIE. Grace is a nice word.

WOYZECK *nods.*

My ma said – when I was packing up – snot hanging out my nose – everyone telling me I was a whore – she said – 'Be careful of the soldiers' – even before – she said 'They're taught to damage.' I said, 'But my one isn't – he's soft.'

WOYZECK. I am soft.

MARIE. He needs love, I said.

WOYZECK. I do need love.

MARIE. And he's a pretty crap soldier by all accounts.

WOYZECK (*laugh*). I am a pretty crap soldier by all accounts.

MARIE *looks at him*.

MARIE. She wanted to get it cut out, said she knew someone who could. My mother – the most pious woman you've ever known – that's when I knew I had to come. With my soft soldier.

WOYZECK. I'd have liked to have met your mother.

MARIE. My ma wouldn't have liked to meet you if I'm honest.

WOYZECK. I know.

MARIE. She'd have tried to cut your balls off no doubt. Most pious woman – fucking hypocrite. That's when I knew – I had to leave. I still remember her you know – plastering the make-up on so as the bruises didn't show. I used to think she did it for my da, but no, she did it for herself. Same as she'd have me abort so as people would still think me a good Catholic girl. People who live their lives just for other people – those are the people I despise the most.

WOYZECK. That's not how I live my life. How we live ours.

MARIE. No. But the truth is – we're too desperate to do anything but live our lives desperately.

WOYZECK *digests this*.

Can you keep it together, Frank? I need you to, she needs you to. I know you're sent away from yourself sometimes but – no more headbutting walls or – we need you. Can you keep it together?

WOYZECK. I hope so.

MARIE *nods*.

They think I ran away. In Belfast. Because I was scared.

MARIE. I'd have been scared. Day after the bomb, wasn't it?

WOYZECK. It was the day after the bomb, yes. But I wasn't scared.

MARIE. Why not?

WOYZECK. Because I'd be happy to die for my country.

MARIE. I fucking wouldn't. Not you for yours or me for mine.

WOYZECK. I ran because I saw my mother.

MARIE. You saw your mum? In Belfast?

WOYZECK. Just walking down the street.

MARIE. And so you followed her?

WOYZECK. She walked quickly. She always – she always walked like everyone watched – and they did – she was a shapely woman –

MARIE. I've seen your picture.

WOYZECK. She led me through these areas – unionist – republican – she didn't care –

MARIE. Were you in uniform?

WOYZECK. I think people shouted, but I didn't notice – she looked beautiful.

MARIE. Mothers always do –

WOYZECK. We ended up on top of this hill – felt like we could see everything –

MARIE. Cave Hill? You walked up Cave Hill? In full uniform? Fuck.

WOYZECK. It was the most beautiful thing.

MARIE. Always want to see everything, don't you?

He kisses her.

WOYZECK. It was beautiful and it gave me hope. And you told me about our child a week later – and I felt blessed. Hopeful.

MARIE. You didn't tell me none of this, by the way. You didn't tell me at all.

WOYZECK. We were blessed that day – I could forgive her and so start fresh. Blessed.

He kisses her again. She pulls away.

And then relents and kisses him.

MARIE. Whatever is in that head of yours.

WOYZECK. Hope.

MARIE. Hope is the way for you, isn't it?

WOYZECK. I'm going to be good for you. Right for you. I know
I – slip – sometimes. But I can set that right. Honestly, I'm
going to try with everything I've got.

MARIE. Okay.

He kisses her a final time.

WOYZECK. They tried to kill the Pope?

MARIE. There you are, you're back with me.

WOYZECK. Why would they kill the Pope?

MARIE. Your guess is as good as mine. Maybe they were
a young mother living in sin who was disappointed she
couldn't wash it all away.

WOYZECK *looks at her.*

No. No. I don't mean that. Or maybe I do. Oh, fuck knows
what I mean. Fuck knows what you do to me.

WOYZECK. I give you hope.

He smiles.

And don't worry. Everything important is a sin.

MARIE *says nothing. And then she laughs.*

MARIE. I don't remember meeting you – I don't remember the
exact moment when I met you – I'm not – but I do remember
how light I felt coming home from meeting – you –

WOYZECK. You danced down the street?

MARIE. No, I did not dance down the street, I'm not one of
those women, but I couldn't stop – my sister said – you can't
stop smiling and I couldn't.

WOYZECK. Do you remember our first kiss?

MARIE. I do remember our first kiss.

WOYZECK. It was so delicate.

MARIE. It was delicate.

WOYZECK. I'd never kissed – or been kissed like it –

MARIE. Me neither.

WOYZECK. I felt transported – like I'd been taken to a new place –

MARIE. It was nice.

WOYZECK. And then we'd go on these walks. You'd take me places.

MARIE. I wanted you to see the beauty of where you were. Belfast is the most beautiful city on earth when you can see it clearly.

WOYZECK. And you'd allow me to see everything.

MARIE. You always want to see everything.

WOYZECK. And in that field –

MARIE. There was more than one field –

WOYZECK. The way you touched me.

MARIE. The way you touched me.

He kisses her. She kisses him back.

WOYZECK. I could feel your love. I've never felt someone's love before.

MARIE. It was nice.

WOYZECK. I could feel you loved me.

MARIE. You felt a lot of other things too.

WOYZECK. It was so beautiful.

MARIE. It was – nice.

He kisses her again.

And then I discovered what I discovered and I was crying and not sure what to do – and you said – you said it was easy – you said I could come with you –

WOYZECK. You should come with me. I'm going to Germany. You should come with me. Germany is safe. We can build a life there.

MARIE. We can build a life there.

WOYZECK. And we have.

MARIE *looks at him and smiles kindly.*

This – I don't mind this place – it's the only place I've felt loved.

MARIE. Do you feel loved?

WOYZECK. Yes.

MARIE. I wish you sounded less sad when you said that.

WOYZECK. Do you feel loved?

MARIE. Yes. I think so. But other times I think...

WOYZECK. What?

MARIE. Other times I'm not sure you know what love is.

WOYZECK. Because my love is sad?

MARIE. Because it's – scary – sometimes.

WOYZECK. Test me. Ask me to do anything. I'd do – I'd do anything for you.

MARIE. I don't want to fucking test you.

WOYZECK. You're testing me now.

MARIE. No. I'm just saying what – how I feel.

WOYZECK (*quoting the* CAPTAIN). The best tests are not announced.

MARIE. You see? You were talking all lovely, and now you're talking all mental. And in a minute you'll slam your head into a fucking – and I'm supposed to just – think what?

WOYZECK. I know what I am, and I know what you are and I know what we mean and I'm going to protect that.

MARIE. What the fuck does that mean?

WOYZECK *looks at her.*

WOYZECK. My mother came to see me once…

MARIE. I know, and you walked up a hill.

WOYZECK. No. She was dead by then.

MARIE. I know. I knew you were talking about a ghost.
I thought she was dead from when you were four. You said
you was in an orphanage from four.

WOYZECK. No. I was in care from four and then she died
when I was – twelve I think.

MARIE. Why did she put you in care?

WOYZECK. She didn't choose to. I was taken from her.

MARIE. For what?

WOYZECK. She was given visitation though, and so she came
to see me and she had a man with her. She took me home to
her house – she wasn't supposed to do that, she asked me to
sneak out, which I did, it wasn't hard. She asked me to watch
while he fucked her. She was quite ill by that point. He paid
her extra I think. She put me in a home at four. Told me she
was coming for me. Told me she'd come for me. I waited.
But that's the only time I ever saw her. I was – nine, I think.
And then when I was twelve. They told me she died.

MARIE. Jesus.

WOYZECK. But I could forgive her – I did forgive her – and
the reason why I was able to was because of all you gave me.
A child. A life. I asked you to come with me – you said yes.

MARIE *says nothing.*

I need to save you because you saved me.

There's a long silence.

MARIE. Frank, that is not a – Jesus.

WOYZECK. Don't focus on the story, focus on the message of
the story.

MARIE *thinks. And then nods. But it's not a true nod.*

MARIE. Then I'll let you have saved me. Saved him. Saved me.

WOYZECK. Thank you.

WOYZECK *nods. He kisses her. She kisses him back.*

MARIE. Maybe if you just slowed down, got some rest.

WOYZECK. I can't sleep. When I close my eyes everything just goes round and round and I hear these strange – fiddles.

MARIE. Maybe if you slowed down –

WOYZECK. Everything just – speaks – and it's so loud, I wonder why everyone else can't hear it – but also I know – no one else can hear it. What do you think that means?

He pauses and looks at her.

MARIE. I don't – know.

WOYZECK. Anyway, all that, it doesn't matter, all that matters is I love you and I'm grateful to you and thank you.

MARIE *says nothing.*

Do you think I love you too much?

MARIE. I don't know.

WOYZECK. But you do think I saved you?

MARIE. Sure.

The two embrace, it holds for a long time, they rotate around, so we see both their faces, she looks scared, he looks overwhelmed.

WOYZECK. I think we're going to be okay.

MARIE. I hope you're right.

Interval.

ACT THREE

Scene One

The flat.

MAGGIE *and* ANDREWS *are having sex. She's riding him.*

MAGGIE. Left a bit.

He concentrates.

Left a bit more.

He concentrates.

Left a bit more.

He throws her over on to her back.

Oh.

ANDREWS. Fuck your left a bit.

MAGGIE. Oh. That's better.

ANDREWS. Fuck you.

MAGGIE. Pull my hair.

He does.

Put your hand over my mouth. Call me a cunt.

He puts his hand over her mouth.

ANDREWS. You're a cunt.

He hollers out in pain.

You bit my hand.

MAGGIE. I'm a cunt. And you're a brute. Fuck me.

ANDREWS. You're a cunt.

MAGGIE. You're a brute.

ANDREWS. You're a cunt.

MAGGIE. You're a brute.

ANDREWS. You're a cunt.

MAGGIE. You're a grunt.

ANDREWS. You're a cunt.

MAGGIE. You're a grunt.

ANDREWS. You're a cunt.

MAGGIE. You're a grunt.

She orgasms.

ANDREWS. You're there.

MAGGIE. I'm there, my lover. I'm there.

ANDREWS. You're there?

MAGGIE. I am.

He orgasms.

They both lie panting on the bed.

Shit.

ANDREWS. Shit.

They both lie panting a bit more.

MAGGIE. You don't know what it is – to be as bored as I am.

ANDREWS. You're fucking bored? You should try being a grunt.

MAGGIE. A grunt is a very good word for you. And cunt is a very good word for me. I think. Sometimes. And then I hope that I'm better than that. I'm probably not. Have you a cigarette?

ANDREWS. She's got a baby.

MAGGIE. If the baby can survive living here it can survive a little smoke. Give me a fag, slag.

ANDREWS *grabs his jeans and pulls out a packet of fags and gives her one. She lights it.*

She smokes it luxuriously.

Jesus. This place…

ANDREWS. Grunts don't get good pay. We're expected to live in barracks. They're not married so she can't live in barracks. I tried it once before. Though I didn't have a kiddie.

MAGGIE. You've got a strong back. This muscle. I don't think my husband has this muscle.

ANDREWS. Squats.

MAGGIE *nods. She touches his back.*

MAGGIE. My husband thinks he might be retarded.

ANDREWS. Woyzeck's not retarded.

MAGGIE. My husband thinks everyone's retarded.

ANDREWS. Everyone hates him. He went AWOL in Belfast. We all had to go look for him. Turned out he – well, you don't want to know where he was hiding. When they found him he was crying. I'm the only one who'll do patrol with him now.

MAGGIE. You don't care. You've got a strong back. You can carry him.

ANDREWS. I don't mind feeling pity. I quite like it.

There's a knocking.

And then more knocking.

You can come through.

He pulls the sheet up over them both.

MARIE *enters the room.* MAGGIE *continues to smoke.*

MARIE. Sorry. He needed his bear.

She looks around for his bear.

ANDREWS *finds it wedged in the bed. He hands it to* MARIE.

MAGGIE. Thank you for not finding this embarrassing, Marie.

MARIE. No.

MAGGIE. And thank you for your hospitality.

MARIE. Sorry, I needed to be inside the flat.

MAGGIE. No. That's quite understandable. You've a child after all.

She looks at MARIE. *She looks at* ANDREWS.

Those envelopes. Still on top of it?

MARIE. Yes.

MAGGIE. I think I may have found you a pram. No promises. One of the girls who's looking to impress me. She won't take any money. May I use your shower? I smell of meat.

MARIE. Yes.

MAGGIE. Though does your shower smell of meat too? Does it rain meat?

MARIE. It doesn't.

MAGGIE. Good-oh.

She walks off to the shower. ANDREWS *watches her go.*

ANDREWS. A fine woman.

MARIE. Yes.

ANDREWS. The eldest I've had.

MARIE. Did she even care – about smoking?

He gets out of bed. He doesn't attempt to cover himself.

ANDREWS. We're very grateful for this –

MARIE. It was not from me you asked permission. For I wouldn't have given it.

ANDREWS. So should I be apologetic to you?

MARIE. Just don't be grateful.

ANDREWS turns and looks at her.

He lifts her head.

ANDREWS. You need a strong man, you know that?

MARIE. Put some clothes on.

ANDREWS *pulls on his trousers, he puts his pants in his pocket.*

ANDREWS. What washing powder do you use?

MARIE. You can fuck off if you think I'll wash your clothes.

ANDREWS. I'll bet he buys you the cheap stuff, right? Omo washing powder, that's the one you want to use.

ANDREWS *looks at her and smiles.*

It really does smell of meat.

WOYZECK *enters the house. He's in full uniform. He looks at* MARIE *and then the half-dressed* ANDREWS. *It looks odd and everyone knows it.*

MARIE. Hi.

WOYZECK. Hi.

ANDREWS. This man I'm allowed to be grateful to, right, Marie?

MARIE. Sure.

ANDREWS. Job done, mate.

WOYZECK. Okay.

WOYZECK *looks at him,* ANDREWS *pulls on his top.*

ANDREWS. She's just washing the sex off her. I'll keep it on me. Time for a drink? It's happy hour in The Lion and Unicorn I think.

WOYZECK *looks at* MARIE *and then* ANDREWS.

WOYZECK. I'm due on shift.

Scene Two

Captain's quarters.

WOYZECK *is gently massaging the* CAPTAIN.

CAPTAIN THOMPSON. I have decided you fascinate me, Woyzeck.

WOYZECK. Do I, sir?

CAPTAIN THOMPSON. Always full of brio. Always full of can-do attitude. The army needs men like you. And yet – there's something missing, isn't there?

WOYZECK. Is there, sir?

CAPTAIN THOMPSON. A missing synapse perhaps – a missing beat in the drum –

WOYZECK. I'm not sure that's true, sir.

CAPTAIN THOMPSON. And I don't just mean your mad fucking dances across Belfast.

WOYZECK. No, sir.

CAPTAIN THOMPSON. Or your illiteracy. You are illiterate, right?

WOYZECK *says nothing.*

Quite crafty, to not let anyone know, how did you do the forms?

WOYZECK. Paid someone.

CAPTAIN THOMPSON. Did you never want to read?

WOYZECK. Yes.

CAPTAIN THOMPSON. Did you never go to school?

WOYZECK. No.

CAPTAIN THOMPSON. Why not?

WOYZECK. People called me thick.

CAPTAIN THOMPSON. If you don't mind me saying, that's a very thick reason not to go.

WOYZECK. I know.

CAPTAIN THOMPSON. Fascinating. You're fascinating. I'm not sure I'll ever get to the bottom of you. Perhaps no man ever will.

WOYZECK. I think I'm quite ordinary, sir.

CAPTAIN THOMPSON. Maybe only the extraordinary think they're ordinary, have you considered that?

WOYZECK's *belly growls.*

Is that your stomach, Woyzeck?

WOYZECK. Yes, sir. Sorry, sir.

CAPTAIN THOMPSON. Diarrhoea?

WOYZECK. No, sir.

CAPTAIN THOMPSON. Because all instances of diarrhoea need to be reported, you know that...

WOYZECK. It's not diarrhoea, sir.

CAPTAIN THOMPSON. Not been eating enough?

WOYZECK. No.

CAPTAIN THOMPSON. Sharing rations with the girl?

WOYZECK. I just am – I'm okay – sir.

CAPTAIN THOMPSON. Has the accommodation problem solved itself, Woyzeck?

WOYZECK. No. And I owe people money, sir.

CAPTAIN THOMPSON. Germans?

WOYZECK. Yes.

The CAPTAIN *looks up at him.*

CAPTAIN THOMPSON. How much do you owe them?

WOYZECK. Four thousand Deutschmarks. I'm behind with rent.

CAPTAIN THOMPSON. You'll soon make that up. Glorious fingers, Woyzeck.

WOYZECK. Thank you, sir.

CAPTAIN THOMPSON. A lot of men are afraid of massage – but as my wife told me – 'The knots need untangling – are you frightened to untangle them?' And I'm not.

WOYZECK. No, sir.

CAPTAIN THOMPSON. I've spent my life overcoming fear. And people think fear is a simplistic thing but actually it's not. It's easy to overcome a fear of death – you just convince yourself that death is inevitable. But the fear of another man's touch. Where does that come from? Do you understand me?

WOYZECK. I do.

CAPTAIN THOMPSON. And I have knots. Knots I'm not afraid to share. Knots caused by years of this. Knots caused by the fact that they only give me Chieftain tanks when I need Challenger ones. Knots caused by the fact that we must constantly play second fiddle to the fucking Belfast mob – we're protecting Europe – they're protecting a peninsula, and yet –

WOYZECK. Yes, sir.

CAPTAIN THOMPSON. The Poles are breaking for freedom, the Pope has been shot, the Soviets are scared, the attack could happen at any moment.

The CAPTAIN *turns so he's looking at* WOYZECK. *He smiles a cruel smile. And then his smile fades.*

You can go lower if you want – with your hands.

WOYZECK. Yes, sir.

CAPTAIN THOMPSON. I got a woman pregnant when I was your age, Woyzeck.

WOYZECK. Did you?

CAPTAIN THOMPSON. I did as expected – we got engaged. And then we both woke up covered in blood. From the legs down. I thought I was bleeding for a moment – I thought my arse had just opened up and was bleeding. Or that my penis had been cut off. Strange, the thoughts you have.

WOYZECK. And then you discovered it was her?

CAPTAIN THOMPSON. Two weeks later, to my great relief, she called the engagement off. I think she knew that I would call it off if she didn't. Lovely body. Terrible face. It wouldn't have been a pleasant marriage. Here's a tip for you, every woman has a good body in a wedding dress, but not many have the face for it. We still exchange Christmas cards.

WOYZECK. That's good.

CAPTAIN THOMPSON. Three years later, she told me the child wasn't even mine. She just decided of everyone she'd slept with, I was the best bet. The child was actually the child of some musician.

WOYZECK. That's interesting.

CAPTAIN THOMPSON. Or a magician. Maybe she said magician. Magician is even worse than musician, wouldn't you say?

WOYZECK. I would.

MAGGIE *enters in the background.*

CAPTAIN THOMPSON. Oh hello, darling, don't mind us?

MAGGIE. I'm the opposite of minding.

CAPTAIN THOMPSON. Wonderful hands – Woyzeck has wonderful hands.

MAGGIE. How very fortunate for you both.

CAPTAIN THOMPSON. How much did you raise today?

MAGGIE. No figures today.

CAPTAIN THOMPSON. She raises a huge amount for charity. Runs ents. Queen of the Naafi, that's what I call her – 'Queen of the Naafi'.

MAGGIE. He flatters me. You flatter me, darling.

CAPTAIN THOMPSON. Queen of the Naafi. Yours to rule over as you wish.

MAGGIE. Well, nice to meet you, Woyzeck.

WOYZECK. You look like someone I know.

MAGGIE. Everyone looks like someone else after a while. It's why dogs look like their owners. Ah, you're the one with the girl in that meat flat, aren't you?

CAPTAIN THOMPSON. Meat flat?

MAGGIE. Extraordinary girl. She has delivered me over five thousand envelopes. Good Catholic girl.

CAPTAIN THOMPSON. Wonderful.

MAGGIE. Well, yes, quite, must get on.

She exits. The CAPTAIN *watches her go.* WOYZECK *does too.*

CAPTAIN THOMPSON. Halte nicht an.

WOYZECK. Sorry, sir?

CAPTAIN THOMPSON. Don't stop, Woyzeck. The massage.

WOYZECK. Ah. Sorry, sir.

He continues to massage.

CAPTAIN THOMPSON. You know what I think life is, Woyzeck? A series of attempts to persuade people to love us. We find someone – man or woman – to love – they love us back – we make them sign a certificate saying they'll do so for ever. Then we have children – and get given certificates saying they love us from the very beginning. Then we just need to persuade them that they do. That the certificate doesn't lie.

WOYZECK. That's interesting, sir.

CAPTAIN THOMPSON. Quis Separabit. Quis Separabit? Love will separate us. Love. Or the fact we aren't loved. I've been looking in your file, Woyzeck. Reading it.

YOUNG WOYZECK *comes out across the stage. He begins a strange dance.*

WOYZECK. Yes, sir.

WOYZECK *tries to copy* YOUNG WOYZECK'*s dance.*

CAPTAIN THOMPSON. Not out of any – professional need – not to worry – just amateur curiosity. I hope you don't mind.

WOYZECK. No, sir.

CAPTAIN THOMPSON. Seven foster families. Three of whom sent you back for being a disruptive influence. You don't seem like a disruptive influence to me?

WOYZECK. They were just trying to make themselves feel better about the fact they didn't like me, sir.

CAPTAIN THOMPSON. Is that so?

WOYZECK. Yes, sir.

CAPTAIN THOMPSON. Because – not to be rude – that sounds like the sort of thing one says to make oneself feel better.

WOYZECK. It doesn't make me feel better. They didn't like me.

CAPTAIN THOMPSON. Ah. Interesting. Yes. I can see how you might feel that. I never worry if someone likes me or not – it's when I feel culpable that I am concerned. You've stopped massaging again.

WOYZECK. Yes, sir, the truth is, I don't feel well at all, sir.

CAPTAIN THOMPSON. Well, at least you're not the Pope, son. At least you're not the Pope.

Scene Three

Doctor's surgery.

WOYZECK *is standing with his top off.*

DOCTOR MARTENS. Did I just see you pissing in the street?

WOYZECK. I'm finding myself getting caught – getting caught –

DOCTOR MARTENS. Do people piss in the street in your country?

WOYZECK. No. Only if – I'm not sure I'm very well. I'm not well. It's these pills – they're making me – I feel all backed up – but I'm pissing and shitting all the time.

ANDREWS. Come back here...

MAGGIE *runs across the space.*

ANDREWS *runs after her. They chase each other around the stage.*

DOCTOR MARTENS. And that's great for you, but – just to say – there's little I can do about that – my experiment, however, as you well know, relies on me being able to monitor your piss. I made very clear, no pissing three hours before visiting me. Your piss now is absolutely useless. I've a good mind to remove you from the trial.

ANDREWS *grabs* MAGGIE, *he wrestles her to the floor.*

WOYZECK. Maybe you should, sir. I'm really not very well.

DOCTOR MARTENS. I've heard things about you, Woyzeck. Things about what you are. Things about what you did.

WOYZECK. What have you heard, sir?

DOCTOR MARTENS. Things.

He looks at WOYZECK *for a long time.*

But there's no time for that. We're late for our presentation...

WOYZECK *looks at the* DOCTOR.

Who leads him through into bright lights.

Scene Four

The flat.

WOYZECK *is looking at his baby.*

WOYZECK. Have you ever seen double nature? When the sun is at its highest point in the sky and it is as if the whole world is on fire. Sometimes – when that's the case, I feel like the whole world is speaking to me.

His MOTHER *stumbles on to stage.*

MOTHER. Frank! Frank! Look at the mess you've made.

The baby laughs. WOYZECK *looks at it, surprised.*

WOYZECK. Why doesn't the God snuff out the sun so the whole world can fall on top of each other in their fornication. Man and woman, man and beast. Why doesn't that happen?

MOTHER. Frank! Look at the fucking mess!

He stands up.

WOYZECK. Maybe man exists because – he's needed – and maybe everything inside man exists because it's needed. We wear clothes because we're ashamed and that's necessary because how else would the tailor make his living. You see? Is that why the world is as the world is? Do you think?

A child emerges from within the crib. It's a young boy. It's YOUNG WOYZECK.

MOTHER. What have you done? What the fuck have you done?

She exits with speed, pulling YOUNG WOYZECK *with her.*

WOYZECK. But then if that's the case we need to find a need – don't we need to find a need? And if you have no need. You don't need me. You don't. And she doesn't need me. And I need to be needed.

He waits a moment. He looks back at the baby.

MARIE *enters in the back of the room.*

I think – the things I saw out there – I had to rescue your mother. I had to rescue her. And I thought that meant I had a need and it doesn't.

MARIE *makes to speak and then holds back.*

You have my eyes, I think. But your eyes have more life in them. And your nose has my shape but it's much more – delicate. And then there's your smile. I think that's like mine too. I see so much of myself in you and it scares me.

MARIE. You shouldn't say those things to her. You shouldn't talk about being scared.

WOYZECK. You're here.

MARIE. You shouldn't – it'll upset her. The things she hears they'll get into her head. She already hears the dying screaming goats.

WOYZECK. She?

MARIE. It'll upset her, Woyzeck.

WOYZECK. Her? I thought he was a he? I thought he was a boy?

MARIE. Did you?

WOYZECK. Little Woyzeck. It's a boy.

MARIE *takes a step back, she knows now he's gone.*

MARIE (*softly*). It's a girl, Frank.

WOYZECK *looks at her. He realises she isn't lying.*

WOYZECK. Is it okay – still to see myself in her – if she's a girl?

MARIE. I don't think so.

WOYZECK. Because I see myself. In her. So clearly.

MARIE. That's only okay if you see that reflection as a good thing.

He kisses her. She pulls away.

WOYZECK. No, I need that.

MARIE. No.

WOYZECK. I do, I need that.

He kisses her again.

MARIE. Please.

WOYZECK. It's so hot.

He kisses her again.

MARIE. Please.

He stops.

He walks away. And then he comes straight back.

Scene Five

And suddenly he's not there and ANDREWS *is.*

ANDREWS. She's not coming, is she?

MARIE. Something must have come up.

ANDREWS. It's fine. I know what I am to her, it's fine.

MARIE. Well, okay then.

ANDREWS. She's had others, you know. She likes them big. Big and thick. I'm okay with that.

He looks at her.

Oh, I almost forgot, I bought you a present.

He opens his bag. He pulls out a packet of Omo washing powder.

It's good stuff.

MARIE. Okay. Shit present, but okay.

ANDREWS. It's actually a really good present – because it's actually useful.

There's a beat. He keeps looking at her.

How is he?

MARIE *says nothing.*

He keeps telling me his dreams, you know, and they started pretty fucking weird but now – last dream he had he stuck a pipe up his urethra and fed the blood to the baby.

MARIE. I don't think he'd want you to tell me that.

ANDREWS. You're not worried?

MARIE *says nothing*.

Or you are worried – just don't trust me to be worried with. I care about him.

MARIE. If you cared about him you wouldn't look at me like that.

ANDREWS. How am I looking at you?

MARIE. I don't know. Wolfishly.

ANDREWS. That's an excellent word. And I apologise. I can't help it.

MARIE. You're just looking at me like that because she's not here. And you want to get your dick wet.

ANDREWS. I'm pretty sure this is the way I've always looked at you.

MARIE. If you cared about him you wouldn't look at me like that. He's your best friend.

ANDREWS. Best? Best would probably be taking it too far. Besides, I already have a best friend.

MARIE *says nothing*.

You'll judge me if I tell you who.

MARIE. What?

ANDREWS. If I told you who my actual best friend is.

MARIE. I don't give a fuck who it is.

ANDREWS. My father. My father is my best friend. He was army too.

MARIE *says nothing. Just stands up and walks around the room*. ANDREWS *watches her arse*.

He was too young for the war but was part of the clean-up.
Finds it funny I'm out here now. Said it made him the man
he was. Discipline, you see, camaraderie. I haven't found it
exactly like that. You have a proper swing in your hips, you
know that? You try and hide it but it's there.

MARIE *says nothing*.

Have you got a best friend? Back home?

MARIE. Of course I do.

ANDREWS. Girl or boy?

MARIE. Girl. Rosie.

ANDREWS. Do you write?

MARIE. She won't answer my letters.

ANDREWS. He did a fucking clever thing, Woyzeck. The rest
of us, their mothers would work at the barracks – cleaners or
cooks – and they'd bring their daughters in for 'socialising'.
They knew what it meant. Their daughters knew what it
meant. But they were dirty and generally ugly Protestants.
The Catholic girls, none of us ever thought. But he… he got
the girl with the swing in her hips.

MARIE *doesn't say anything*.

How did it even happen?

MARIE. I think you should leave.

ANDREWS. He must have been out of uniform. If you didn't
know he was army.

MARIE *nods*.

Not supposed to do that. Go on, what did he have about him?
I'll stop looking at your arse. Go on. I've been pretty fucking
humiliated today, don't throw me out.

MARIE *thinks*.

MARIE. He seemed to see things other people didn't. He saw –
fun – in the world.

ANDREWS. I see fun in the world.

MARIE. He made this joke – about – the sea – about the way
the sea moves. I can't remember it. But it was beautiful.
I liked him. I like him. I'm going to check on the baby.

ANDREWS *looks her up and down.*

ANDREWS. I went East the other day. Went through Berlin.
Fucking great. Met a dancing monkey. Dressed as a soldier.
Felt sorry for the poor cunt. All the things he could be and
they dress him as a soldier. And then they made him dance.

MARIE. Sounds inhumane.

ANDREWS. It was a monkey, who gives a shit, but the dance
was quite –

He starts to do the dance.

It was sort of all groin, you know? Like –

He pivots his pelvis backwards and forwards.

But when his arse would go back he'd sort of twitch it.

He twitches his arse at the extremes of the pivot. She laughs.

See? That's fun in the world. You just laughed. It was sort of
erotic. But could he help that, no? It was just how he danced.
Fun, right? Like he sees.

MARIE. Yes.

*He mimics it again. But he knows she's not totally convinced.
She sort of half-laughs.*

ANDREWS. Are you okay, Marie? Does he scare you? Don't
you need to think about your daughter? If he scares you.

MARIE. Please. Just get out of our flat.

Scene Six

WOYZECK *is sitting on the street.*

The song from Act One is reprised – but it's distorted, wrong.

SINGER.
>War clouds gather over ev'ry land,
>Our flag is threaten'd east and west.
>Nations that we've shaken by the hand
>Our bold resources try to test
>They thought they found us sleeping
>Thought us unprepar'd.

WOYZECK *looks one way.*

ANDREWS *and* MAGGIE/MOTHER *are having sex.*

>Because we have our party wars,
>But Englishmen unite when they're call'd to fight
>The battle for Old England's common cause,
>The battle for Old England's common cause.
>So when we say that England's master,
>Remember who has made her so.

WOYZECK *looks back –* ANDREWS *turns* MAGGIE/MOTHER *over in bed.*

And suddenly it's MARIE *that's riding* ANDREWS *instead.*

WOYZECK *looks at it for a long time.*

WOYZECK *walks over.*

He touches MARIE*'s body.*

He puts his thumb in MARIE*'s mouth. She lets him.*

He gently puts his hand on her neck.

He gently puts his hand on her breast. He feels the way the nipple feels in his hand.

She keeps riding ANDREWS.

Donation envelopes fall from the ceiling.

WOYZECK *tries to catch one of them.*

And then ANDREWS *turns* MARIE *over and suddenly* MAGGIE/MOTHER *is riding him again.*

MAGGIE/MOTHER. It'll soon be over, Frank. It'll soon be over.

WOYZECK *looks horrified.*

CAPTAIN THOMPSON. Is this your post?

He turns to see CAPTAIN THOMPSON *looking at him. He looks back at* ANDREWS *and* MAGGIE/MOTHER. *They've gone.*

WOYZECK. Yes, sir.

CAPTAIN THOMPSON. You're manning it alone?

WOYZECK. I think so, sir.

CAPTAIN THOMPSON. Who's supposed to be on patrol with you?

WOYZECK. I don't know, sir.

CAPTAIN THOMPSON. Are you drunk?

WOYZECK. No. I'm not well.

CAPTAIN THOMPSON. You seem drunk.

WOYZECK. Because I'm not well. I've started peeing strange colours.

CAPTAIN THOMPSON. What colours are you peeing?

WOYZECK. Sorry?

CAPTAIN THOMPSON. Welche Farben pissen Sie?

WOYZECK. My head hurts.

CAPTAIN THOMPSON. Then come here. It'll be soon be over. Come here and let me hold you until it is.

WOYZECK. What?

CAPTAIN THOMPSON. Get your shit together, do you understand that? You're drunk. You're on a charge.

WOYZECK. What? No. I'm here for help.

CAPTAIN THOMPSON. You're where for help?

There's the sound of guns from off.

WOYZECK. Germany. I came to Germany to get help. We all did. Didn't we all? We all came here for that.

CAPTAIN THOMPSON. Everyone's worried about us, did you know that? Everyone's worried the British are getting sloppy. The CIA, Nato, the Soviets are rubbing their hands with glee. We've seen reports from the KGB, from the Foreign Military Intelligence of the Soviet General Army, the Intelligence Department of the East German National People's Army. These are important things. These are important things.

WOYZECK. I've come to you. I see you, sir. I want some help from you, sir.

CAPTAIN THOMPSON. I am not here to help you. What the fuck do you think I am? I am not here to help you. I am here to combat the peril from the East. I am here to – fucking rotation – you think this is easy – they've given me the wrong fucking tanks, you understand? Get out of here. I'll do your shift. I'll protect us all. They could come at any time, Woyzeck. We must be prepared.

Scene Seven

The bright lights come back.

The bright lights are overbearing.

WOYZECK *is in a lecture theatre beside* DOCTOR MARTENS *and a cat, he struggles to see who's out there and what's going on.*

DOCTOR MARTENS. Meine Herren, ich bin auf dern Dach wie David, als er die Bathseba sah; aber ich sehe nichts als die culs de Paris der Mädchenpension im Garten trocknen.

WOYZECK. I don't understand what you're saying.

DOCTOR MARTENS. Meine Herren, wir sind an der wichtigen Frage über das Verhältnis des Subjekts zum Objekt. Wenn wir nur eins von den Dingen nehmen, worin sich die organische Selbstaffirmation des Göttlichen, auf einem so hohen Standpunkte, manifestiert, und ihre Verhältnisse zum Raum, zur Erde, zum Planetarischen untersuchen, meine Herren, wenn ich diese Katze zum Fenster hinauswerfe: wie wird diese Wesenheit sich zum centrum gravitationis gemä§ ihrem eigenen Instinkt verhalten?

He picks up and throws the cat out of the window.

He, Woyzeck – Woyzeck!

WOYZECK. Did you just throw a cat out of the window?

DOCTOR MARTENS. Ei, ei! Schön, Woyzeck! Was seh' ich, meine Herren, die neue Spezies Hasenlaus, eine schöne Spezies É.

Meine Herren, das Tier hat keinen wissenschaftlichen Instinkt É Sie können dafür was anders sehen. Sehen Sie: der Mensch; bemerken Sie die Wirkung, fühlen Sie einmal: Was ein ungleicher Puls! Da und die Augen!

WOYZECK. Why aren't you worried about the cat?

DOCTOR MARTENS. Courage, Woyzeck, noch ein Paar Taye und dunn ists fertis, fuhlen sis, meine Herren, fullen sir. Apropos, Woyzeck, beweg den Herren doch einmal die Ohren! Ich hab' es Ihnen schon zeigen wollen, zwei Muskeln sind bei ihm tätig. Bestie, soll ich dir die Ohren bewegen?

He wiggles WOYZECK*'s ears. The class laugh.* WOYZECK
looks at them.

WOYZECK. Are they laughing at me?

DOCTOR MARTENS. Willst du's machen wie die Katze? So,
meine Herren! Das sind so Übergänge zum Esel, häufig auch
die Folge weiblicher Erziehung und die Muttersprache.
Wieviel Haare hat dir die Mutter zum Andenken schon
ausgerissen aus Zärtlichkeit? Sie sind dir ja ganz dünn
geworden seit ein paar Tagen.

WOYZECK. I don't understand why they're laughing. Why are
they laughing? And why is no one concerned about the cat?

And suddenly MARIE *is standing there instead of the*
DOCTOR.

MARIE. Bestie, soll ich dir die Ohren bewegen? Willst du's
machen wie die Katze? So, meine Herren! Das sind so
Übergänge zum Esel, häufig auch die Folge weiblicher
Erziehung und die Muttersprache. Wieviel Haare hat dir die
Mutter zum Andenken schon ausgerissen aus Zärtlichkeit?
Sie sind dir ja ganz dünn geworden seit ein paar Tagen. Ja,
die Erbsen, meine Herren!

Scene Eight

The flat. MAGGIE *faces* MARIE.

MAGGIE. He's not here.

MARIE. No.

MAGGIE. Good. I do worry – you know – when they get attached. I don't encourage it, detachment is what's expected and if they can't deliver on that then I consider it their problem.

MARIE. Did you invite him?

MAGGIE. Yes.

MARIE. But you're pleased he didn't come?

MAGGIE. Extremely. With these grunts it's best they tire of you as you tire of them but the issue needs testing. I invited him three times, once here, once somewhere else, I didn't show to the first two, on the third time I came, and I'm delighted he isn't here.

MARIE. I'm not sure I understand.

MAGGIE. I wouldn't expect you to. Attractive, though, don't you think? Meaty.

MARIE. Yes.

MAGGIE. Your Woyzeck – also very attractive. Wonderful noble features. I sort of want to sculpt him in clay. Or bronze.

MARIE. Bronze?

MAGGIE *looks at her. She looks around the room.*

MAGGIE. You look like you're packing.

MARIE. You can see that?

MAGGIE. Making a run for it?

MARIE. No.

MAGGIE. Leaving Germany before Germany turns on you. Very sensible I'm sure.

MARIE. Germany is not going to turn on me.

MAGGIE. The Pope's been shot – who knows what's going to happen?

MARIE. I don't really think about things like that.

MAGGIE. I do. And – well, here's the thing – maybe because of the attempt on the Pope – I woke last night and I suddenly had this huge concern that you were stealing from me. Well, from the Church.

MARIE. Sorry?

MAGGIE. I was actually quite angry with myself – that I hadn't kept a closer eye upon you. And then I come here and see you making a run for it.

MARIE. I wouldn't steal. I'm Catholic.

MAGGIE. You're living in sin in a Muslim butcher's shop. I would hardly consider that living by the Commandments, would you?

MARIE. You're an adulteress.

MAGGIE. I'm adventurous. I love my husband.

MARIE. I haven't stolen from you.

MAGGIE. I went to Oxford with a girl like you. Bright as a button. By which I don't mean intelligence, she just lit everywhere – people seemed to like her.

She looks at MARIE.

State-school education. Swindon I believe. Have you ever visited Swindon? Probably not, you barely left Ireland, I'm guessing.

MARIE. We went to London once. It wasn't a good trip.

MAGGIE. Anyway, my point is, everyone – in the first year – had her as the girl most likely to succeed – she'd had to try so hard to get there – Swindon to Oxford is not a long trip geographically – but intellectually – wow. We thought she could be the next Prime Minister, anything. And then we realised that by getting to Oxford she'd exhausted herself, she had nothing left to give. We watched her wilt like a flower.

She didn't come back for the second year. Drowned herself in a lake in fact.

MARIE. I didn't go to Oxford. I'm not going to drown myself.

MAGGIE. The trouble is, you haven't collected as much as my other girls. And I do need the money in order so that my life can have impact, you understand? And I thought it might be because your baby screams a lot and you smell of meat, but then I had another thought – people must pity you. So then I considered maybe you'd collected more and skimmed it.

MARIE. The first thing I'd do if I had any money is move out of here.

MAGGIE. You *are* moving out of here.

MARIE. No. Not like that.

MAGGIE. Well, I've no way of proving it. So you're safe.

She looks at MARIE *carefully.*

But – I think it'd be better for both of us if you were to return me the envelopes.

MARIE. You can trust me.

MAGGIE. I like you, you know that? I really like you. Despite myself. Do say goodbye before you leave.

Scene Nine

WOYZECK *sits looking at the Omo washing powder.*

WOYZECK. Marie? Marie.

He tears open the box and begins to pour it on the floor.

Marie? Marie.

MARIE. Woyzeck?

MAGGIE/MOTHER. Woyzeck.

ANDREWS. Woyzeck.

MAGGIE/MOTHER. Woyzeck. I love you.

WOYZECK. You love me.

MAGGIE/MOTHER. But you need to be doing more.

LANDLORD. The money, Woyzeck.

WOYZECK. What?

LANDLORD. You owe me money, Woyzeck.

WOYZECK. I do.

CAPTAIN THOMPSON. I increasingly believe life is about disturbing those who'd put you in a bucket. Raise your eyes, Woyzeck, and count the small gang of your oppressors who are only strong through the blood they suck from you and through your arms which you lend them unwillingly.

WOYZECK. Marie? MARIE? MARIE?

He nods. He nods again.

I am. Doing more. I'm building something. I'm building a family, do you understand? I'm building something to love, do you understand that.

A baby cries.

And then he pours the washing powder into his mouth.

His mouth begins to foam.

He coughs. He coughs again.

He vomits on to the floor.

And then falls on to the floor.

And then WOYZECK *lies still.*

Scene Ten

WOYZECK *lies asleep on the floor.* CAPTAIN THOMPSON *enters. He looks at his body, surprised.*

DOCTOR MARTENS. Shhh. He's sleeping.

CAPTAIN THOMPSON. But that's Woyzeck?

DOCTOR MARTENS. Yes. (*Checks his notes.*) Yes. Woyzeck. I find it easier to know people by numbers. I think you do too.

CAPTAIN THOMPSON. Why's he sleeping?

DOCTOR MARTENS. I can't quite fathom it.

CAPTAIN THOMPSON. It's so interesting watching the sleeping man, do you think there's something you can see in their faces? Something that otherwise might not be there.

DOCTOR MARTENS. Interesting question – if I was to study this face I would say this man... He is a square-basher, he is an empty headpiece.

CAPTAIN THOMPSON. He runs through the world like an open razor, you could cut yourself on him. He rushes about as if he had a regiment of castrates to shave and would be hung if he didn't get them completely entirely clean. He's stirring. No, he's sleeping. No, he's stirring.

WOYZECK *wakes, he looks around himself. He sees them staring down at him.*

WOYZECK. I fell asleep.

DOCTOR MARTENS. You say that like you have no culpability for doing so?

WOYZECK. I've been so tired...

DOCTOR MARTENS. Sleeping is an active act. You chose to fall asleep. Have you pissed yet?

He stands up. He looks at them both. They look back.

WOYZECK. You were watching me sleep.

CAPTAIN THOMPSON. We were.

WOYZECK. Studying me.

DOCTOR MARTENS. It is the greatest gift of being a human, the ability to study others and draw conclusions.

WOYZECK. Is it?

DOCTOR MARTENS. For instance, take my friend here, Captain – ?

CAPTAIN THOMPSON. Thompson.

DOCTOR MARTENS. Thompson. You have a bloated fat neck, Captain. Have you considered that you might be heading for apoplexia cerebri?

CAPTAIN THOMPSON. I haven't.

DOCTOR MARTENS. You might get lucky and only be half-paralysed. Or you might be luckier still and it only affect the brain and so your body rots for lack of imagination.

CAPTAIN THOMPSON. We were talking about the boy.

DOCTOR MARTENS. But luckiest yet would be if your tongue is partially paralysed. The experiments we could conduct. They'd be immortal. Maybe that's why you're here – immortality.

CAPTAIN THOMPSON. I do have such melancholy. I am melancholic. If I see my coat hanging on the wall I burst into tears.

The DOCTOR *takes him in his arms.*

Then they both turn and look at WOYZECK *with smiles.*

DOCTOR MARTENS. What did you dream of, on my floor?

CAPTAIN THOMPSON. Those you fear or those that hold no fear? Those you love or those you hate?

DOCTOR MARTENS. Did you see your future?

CAPTAIN THOMPSON. What does your future contain? Other than loneliness.

WOYZECK. I don't want to be here.

He stands and walks from the room.

DOCTOR MARTENS. You can't just leave. You came to us.
We're at the edge of modern medicine here. Our experiments
have proved fruitful.

WOYZECK. What have you given me?

DOCTOR MARTENS. Bestie, soll ich dir die Ohren bewegen?
Willst du's machen wie die Katze? So, meine Herren! Das
sind so Übergänge zum Esel, häufig auch die Folge weiblicher
Erziehung und die Muttersprache. Wieviel Haare hat dir die
Mutter zum Andenken schon ausgerissen aus Zärtlichkeit? Sie
sind dir ja ganz dünn geworden seit ein paar Tagen.

WOYZECK. What have you? What have you given me?

DOCTOR MARTENS. We're calling it the Human Growth
Hormone. We're very excited about what it might do.

WOYZECK. I don't want to be here.

CAPTAIN THOMPSON. But there's so much we want to know.
Have you found any hairs from someone else's beard in your
soup recently, Woyzeck?

WOYZECK. What?

CAPTAIN THOMPSON. Beard hairs in your soup. Not your
own. Found them.

WOYZECK *turns and looks at them both. And then walks
away.*

That fellow makes me dizzy. How fast the big rascal runs,
groping like a spider's shadow, the little one running after.
The big one is the thunder and the little one the lightning.
Ha! Grotesque. Grotesque. Has my neck really swollen?

DOCTOR MARTENS. Have you ever considered a medical
trial, Captain?

Scene Eleven

WOYZECK *stumbles down the street.*

WOYZECK. Dance, everyone – on and on –

MAGGIE. Please don't talk to me – not in the street.

WOYZECK *looks up, he had no idea he was talking to her, but he immediately recognises her. And then he shuts his eyes.*

WOYZECK. Gone off with a soldier. And polished his gun –

MAGGIE. The meat soldier, am I right? Get the fuck away from me.

WOYZECK. The devil takes the one and lets the other go. But which does he choose? Which does the devil choose?

MAGGIE *grabs him and hisses in his ear.*

MAGGIE/MOTHER. Whatever you think you've got, I can take it all away.

WOYZECK. But I have nothing –

MAGGIE *turns back and this time she has* YOUNG WOYZECK *in her hand.*

MAGGIE/MOTHER. Do you know what you are?

WOYZECK. No.

YOUNG WOYZECK. No.

MAGGIE/MOTHER. Do you know what you are?

WOYZECK. Nothing?

And then from the ceiling comes a hard shower of green pills.

They rain down mercilessly.

MAGGIE/MOTHER. You want to watch Mummy?

WOYZECK. No.

MAGGIE/MOTHER. You want to watch Mummy?

YOUNG WOYZECK. No.

MAGGIE/MOTHER. You should watch Mummy?

YOUNG WOYZECK. No.

MAGGIE/MOTHER. Mummy would like it if you watched Mummy?

YOUNG WOYZECK. Okay.

MAGGIE/MOTHER. You don't look like me. If I hadn't pushed you out. You don't look like me. Too much self-pity, I think. On your face. You don't look like me. But then I suppose dogs grow to look like their owners. Or is it owners look like their dogs?

WOYZECK. I'm not afraid.

YOUNG WOYZECK. I'm not afraid.

MAGGIE/MOTHER. You should be. You should be afraid of everything. Keep watching, Woyzeck. Who else do you think he's fucking? A dick like that, he'll fuck anything. You used to have her, now you've got nothing. Why? You're right, you're nothing.

Scene Twelve

And then MAGGIE *is not there and* ANDREWS *is.*

WOYZECK *looks at him suspiciously.*

ANDREWS *picks up a gun and twists it around. He performs triumphant arcs with it.*

WOYZECK *doesn't have a gun.*

WOYZECK. It's my birthday.

ANDREWS. Is it? I thought you had that a few months ago.

WOYZECK. Today I am twenty-four years old. And that seems old enough.

ANDREWS. No, I remember it. It's not your fucking birthday. I got you a card and a pot of Bovril from the Naafi.

WOYZECK. Twenty-four years old.

ANDREWS. You're drunk, my friend.

WOYZECK. I don't drink. My dad drunk. I don't drink.

ANDREWS. Well then, someone has done something to your head.

WOYZECK. I have a picture of Jesus, and a Bible, that's all I have from her.

ANDREWS. From who?

WOYZECK. And inside she wrote –

'Lord, as you were red and sore
So let my heart be for evermore.'

What do you think that means?

ANDREWS. I don't know.

WOYZECK. I think it means she wants pain. Deserves pain. Feels like she may deserve pain. Well, she can't feel anything any more, can she?

ANDREWS. Woyzeck, you need to lie down.

WOYZECK. You were my only friend.

ANDREWS. Was I?

WOYZECK. Yes.

ANDREWS. You weren't my only friend.

WOYZECK. You were my only friend and now you've spit on me.

ANDREWS. You're not making sense.

WOYZECK. You were my only friend and she was the only thing I ever loved. The only thing I ever loved.

ANDREWS. Whatever you think happened…

WOYZECK. I can smell her on you.

ANDREWS. Are you having a joke?

WOYZECK. No.

ANDREWS. Are you fucking joking me?

WOYZECK. No.

ANDREWS. Do you know what you're accusing me of?

WOYZECK. Yes.

WOYZECK *charges at him,* ANDREWS *sends* WOYZECK *hard into the wall.*

ANDREWS. Do you know why I liked you? Because you were a little dogshit. Whenever I was feeling crap about myself – whenever I thought I was the shit – I'd always think there was always the dogshit – dogshit is always worse than shit, isn't it?

WOYZECK *swings,* ANDREWS *counters, he hits him repeatedly. Hard penetrating thumps.* ANDREWS *is a better fighter than* WOYZECK.

And then you got her. Her. Will you look at her. You don't deserve her. That's what you're realising. Not that I've done anything wrong just that – you fucking have. Thinking you deserved that. Have you seen that arse? You think you deserve that arse? Dogshit like you. No, mate. No.

WOYZECK *tries to come back,* ANDREWS *slams him hard on to the floor. He kicks him repeatedly.*

I'm kicking you – not because I want to – but because you need to learn a lesson.

He kicks him again.

Don't you understand? Don't you understand it? I can fuck who I like, I deserve to fuck her. Because that's the good bit. And what is this life without the good bits?

He kicks him again.

Fucking hell. Fuck you. You've made me feel shit. Fuck you for making me feel shit. I'm not ashamed of that.

He walks away.

He leaves WOYZECK *on the floor.*

MOTHER *walks onstage.*

She looks at his body.

She makes an odd noise with her mouth.

MOTHER. I never loved you.

She straddles him.

She starts to undress him.

She starts to undress herself.

She lifts his face so that he can drink from her breast.

He does so.

She cradles him.

And as she cries, he cries too.

ACT FOUR

WOYZECK *is pulling* MARIE *across the stage*.

WOYZECK. I've somewhere to show you.

MARIE. Okay.

WOYZECK. You like the things I show you.

MARIE. Woyzeck, this is what we talked about, you're not yourself.

WOYZECK. You're wrong. I actually feel really clear.

MARIE. Why have you bought your gun with you?

WOYZECK. I don't know. It's the strangest thing – I thought I'd lost it and then I hadn't.

MARIE. You're not supposed to have that gun out of uniform. Don't even think about selling it.

WOYZECK. Why would I sell it?

MARIE. You can't make another mistake.

WOYZECK. No. I've made too many mistakes. I'm not selling the gun.

MARIE. So what are you doing with it?

WOYZECK. Nothing.

MARIE. You're scaring me now, Woyzeck.

WOYZECK. I seem to scare you all the time. I have decided to not be scared of scaring you. I've decided it's okay.

MARIE. It's not okay to scare me.

WOYZECK. It is if it's all I can do.

He looks at her. He pulls her roughly.

MARIE. I just think you might need a bit of help. I've been talking to some people.

WOYZECK. I don't need help. I'm clear.

MARIE. You're a father – you need to be strong –

WOYZECK. I am strong.

MARIE. And at the moment I feel like –

WOYZECK. Have you heard me, Marie? I used to only care what you felt like – but now I don't – now I don't care much at all – you can feel like anything and I won't mind.

MARIE. Have you bought that gun because you want to fucking shoot me?

WOYZECK. No.

MARIE. So you just want to scare me with it?

WOYZECK. Why is it all about you?

MARIE. Are you going to shoot yourself? Are you going to shoot yourself in front of me?

WOYZECK. No.

MARIE. It's not some fucking thing you've got inside your head?

WOYZECK. No.

MARIE. Why have you bought the fucking gun then?

WOYZECK *looks at her.*

WOYZECK. Forget about the gun.

MARIE *looks at him and nods.*

MARIE. And where are we going?

WOYZECK. I don't know.

MARIE. You don't know?

WOYZECK. We're going somewhere where we can see everything.

MARIE. In a wood? Good luck with that.

WOYZECK. We're going somewhere where I can tell you about love.

MARIE. Okay.

WOYZECK. Because I don't think you understand love.

MARIE. I don't understand love?

WOYZECK. You don't understand my love. I love you more than I've ever loved anything. I love you more than our child. Loads more. Everyone says you love your child in a way that you've never loved anything – but I've never – I could never love anything as much as I love you.

MARIE *looks at him gently. She half-melts.*

MARIE. Woyzeck. There's some things I need to say. I've spoken to my ma, she'll have me back and the baby – and you can visit and we'll start to work again – once you're a little better – we'll start to work again –

WOYZECK. No, you're not leaving –

MARIE. When you're right – you'll follow us – I can work – my ma can look after the baby – we can live well – because this –

He pulls her back.

WOYZECK. No, you're not leaving.

MARIE. Woyzeck, are you hearing me? I'm not saying I want us to finish, I'm saying I want us to start again. A new life, away from the army, soon as you can afford to buy yourself out – and we'll get you right –

WOYZECK. I am right.

MARIE. I can help you, Woyzeck. I can. And I will. Look at me. I'm the one that does care. That does love. If you love me, you should feel my love for you. The others – they're just – they are only strong through the – blood they suck from you and through your arms which you – lend them unwillingly.

WOYZECK. I don't understand.

MARIE. I'm going to go. I'm going to pack up and go and then when you're well again and out of this fucking army you're going to follow me and we will live a life –

She makes to walk away. He pulls her back.

Can you get your hands off me?

WOYZECK. I can't lose you.

MARIE. Are you not listening to me? You aren't.

WOYZECK. I need you to stay here. It will be better. I can be better. I promise.

MARIE. You won't get well here. You can't.

WOYZECK *blows red.*

WOYZECK. You will fucking stay here, you will fucking stay here, you will fucking stay here.

MARIE. You see? You see what this place has done to you. This place is sick. And – I don't like it here and nor does he.

WOYZECK. She.

MARIE. He. Your son. Your son doesn't like it here.

WOYZECK. I have a daughter. That's all I have. I have you and your daughter – our daughter – and I love you so much –

MARIE *makes to walk away again,* WOYZECK *pulls her back, he pins her to the floor.*

MARIE. You see, when you do that I start to doubt you do love me.

WOYZECK. I have a daughter and you and I love you.

MARIE (*firing back. Colder now*). No. No. I see it now. You're like those twelve-year-old boys, you don't love me, you want to own me.

WOYZECK. No.

MARIE. You want to put me in your books, in your jars, keep me in your jars then take me out to wank on.

WOYZECK. No.

MARIE *pulls away.*

MARIE. You don't love me. I followed you to Germany. To this stinking shithole. And you don't love me.

WOYZECK *picks her up and slams her down on the ground.*

Does that feel like love to you?

WOYZECK. That man… with that man. Of all the men. That man.

MARIE. What fucking… I don't know what you have inside your head.

WOYZECK. The only one who was ever kind to me. And he was lying. And you lied with him.

MARIE. Who the fuck are you talking about?

WOYZECK. I can see it – I can still see it – I can still see you fucking him.

MARIE. This is bullshit. I've not fucked anything other than you and I've barely fucked you.

WOYZECK. I can see you – and him – and him – and you.

MARIE. Fuck you.

WOYZECK. Now I see.

MARIE. See what? There's nothing to see.

WOYZECK. The way – the things I have inside my head for you –

MARIE. You don't have anything inside your head for me. You only have you inside your head. It's your fucking head.

WOYZECK. I love you.

MARIE. You don't. You can't.

WOYZECK. I love you. You're all I have.

MARIE. You don't have me any more.

WOYZECK. I love you.

MARIE. Some fucking love. Get your hands off me.

WOYZECK *puts his hands around her neck.*

WOYZECK. I'm doing this because I love you.

She tries to struggle but he's stronger. He's really strong.

I'm doing this because I love you. I'm doing this because I love you. I'm doing this because I love you. I'm doing this because I love you. I'm doing this because I love you.

I'm doing this because I love you. I'm doing this because I love you. I'm doing this because I love you.

She dies.

And there's a long silence.

WOYZECK *stands up. He walks around. He returns to her.*

There you see, now you're mine.

He touches her face, he recoils away, he touches her face again, he smiles.

And you look so beautiful, so perfect. Look at how beautiful and perfect you look now. I wish you could fucking see. I wish you could fucking see this.

He pounds his head against the floor.

You can fucking see this.

He pounds his head again, blood starts coming from a wound on the top of his head.

The lips need be redder still. The wanton lips need be redder still. What a treat for the lips.

He smears his blood on her lips.

Can you taste me?

And then he sits back.

Can you taste me?

He starts to cry.

I want you to taste me. I want to know what I taste like. Because when I taste me all I can taste is blood.

He just sits back.

But you should. You should taste my love. You should taste my love…

He smears more blood on her lips.

I think you might taste something better if you taste me. It's one of the things I love about you – you are very – you see what's there. And you see it in a nicer way.

There's perfect silence as he just sits there beside her body.

And he starts to make noises with his mouth that are only very very slight.

And then he goes back to silence again.

This is pure unadulterated grief. And pain.

Blood drips down from the gash on his forehead.

He wipes it just before it reaches his eye.

Does this mean I loved you more? I think this means I loved you more. I think this means I loved you most. The best tests – the best tests are not announced.

He suddenly slams his head down again.

And then he slams his head down again.

He repeatedly slams his head into the ground.

And then he stops again.

I'm sorry.

And then he picks up his gun.

Things happened in the wrong order.

And he thinks a moment.

Maybe this is why I bought the gun. I don't know. I don't know why I did anything.

And then he shoots himself.

And then there is nothing.

Epilogue

YOUNG WOYZECK *enters the stage. He looks around himself. He begins to clean.*

He wipes up all the blood.

He covers the bodies.

And then a SINGER *appears behind him and starts to sing.*

SINGER.
> The sun had set behind yon hills,
> Across yon dreary moor,
> Weary and lame, a boy there came
> Up to a farmer's door
> 'Can you tell me if any there be
> That will give me employ,
> To plough and sow, and reap and mow,
> And be a farmer's boy?
>
> 'My father is dead, and Mother is left
> With five children, great and small;
> And what is worse for Mother still,
> I'm the oldest of them all.
> Though little, I'll work as hard as a Turk,
> If you'll give me employ,
> To plough and sow, and reap and mow,
> And be a farmer's boy.

He looks down on the floor.

He starts to chalk it out.

As he chalks it, things start to appear.

Around him and behind him.

The stage becomes an exact replica of how it was in the prologue. Only this time there's two bodies. And somehow they fit into the gaps in the staging.

And if that you won't me employ,
One favour I've to ask, –
Will you shelter me, till break of day,
From this cold winter's blast?
At break of day, I'll trudge away
Elsewhere to seek employ,
To plough and sow, and reap and mow,
And be a farmer's boy.'

'Come, try the lad,' the mistress said,
'Let him no further seek.'
'O, do, dear Father!' the daughter cried,
While tears ran down her cheek
'He'd work if he could, so 'tis hard to want food,
And wander for employ;
Don't turn him away, but let him stay,
And be a farmer's boy.'

YOUNG WOYZECK *looks down at what he's done. And
then he sits down beside* WOYZECK*'s corpse, with his back
to the audience and he stays there.*

And when the lad became a man,
The good old farmer died,
And left the lad the farm he had,
And his daughter for his bride.
The lad that was, the farm now has,
Oft smiles, and thinks with joy
Of the lucky day he came that way,
To be a farmer's boy.

The lights suddenly go off.

There's a sound of a baby crying.